Popcorns,
Bobbles & Puffs
to Crochet

Popcorns, Bobbles & Puffs to Crochet

The Visual Guide to
Everything You Need to Know

Lindy Zubairy

QUARTO PRESS

A QUARTO BOOK

Published in 2016 by
Quarto Press
6 Blundell Street
London N7 9BH
www.quartoknows.com

ISBN: 978-0-85762-149-8

QUAR. PPBC

Senior Editor: Julia Shone
Art Editor and Designer: Julie Francis
Photographer: Phil Wilkins
Pattern Checker: Leonie Morgan
Proofreader: Eleanor Van Zandt
Indexer: Helen Snaith
Creative Director: Moira Clinch
Publisher: Paul Carslake

Colour separation in Singapore by Pica Digital
Pte Limited
Printed in China by 1010 Printing Limited

Quarto is the authority on a wide range of topics.

Quarto educates, entertains and enriches the lives of
our readers — enthusiasts and lovers of hands-on living.

www.quartoknows.com

CONTENTS

The Classroom 8

Yarns and Hooks   10
Reading Patterns   12
Basic Techniques   16
What are Bobbles, Puffs and Popcorns?   22
Getting the Size Right   24
Finishing Your Work   26

Welcome to Lindy's World   6
About This Book   6

The Techniques 30

Bobbles   **32**
Bricking   34
Granny Flower   36
Bobdala   38
Bobble Bumps   39
Bobble Berries   40
Diabobs   41
Polkabobs   42
Long and Leaning   44
Windmills   46

Popcorns   **48**
Scattered Corn   50
Corn Rows   51
Popcorn with Ribs   52
Pop Circles   53
Poptarsia   54
Popcorn Patterning   56
Popcorn Peonies   57
Flopcorns   58
Picorns   60
Popcorn Tulips   61

Puffs   **62**
Bricked Puffs   64
Dipped Puffs   65
Puff Chevron   66
Puffs of Air   67
Puff Cushion   68
Puff Balls   70
Puffs on the Side   71
Spiked Puffs   72
Solomon's Puffs   74
Bullion Stitch   75

The Projects 76

Puff Ball and Berry Rug   78
Puff Bolster Cushion   83
Puff Ball Bag   86
Diamond Popcorn Cowl   91

Common Abbreviations and Index   94
Credits and Video Tutorial Links   96

Welcome to Lindy's World

We each arrive at crochet down different paths, finding solace and satisfaction in its stitches. For me, crochet is an absorbing escape from cares, an indulgence for my senses, an outlet for my creativity and a social networking platform! Through learning and teaching crochet I have met so many people who have shared their wisdom, their stories, their advice and their insights.

I have a hundred crochet projects on the go, it seems. I get a real buzz from learning new stitches and techniques and incorporating them in my designs, and I never leave home without a hook and a hank. I find that crocheting in public often has a friendly effect on people around me who would normally not speak. I've whiled away a lot of downtime on crowded public transport, on the beach, in hospital waiting rooms, you name it ... either happily crocheting or equally happily chatting to a stranger about it and other crafts that come up in conversation.

This book assumes you've already had a dabble at crochet and want to move on to the next level. It is two things (at least) – an improver manual and a brief stitch dictionary. I hope it's an inspiration, as well.

About This Book

With its informative, colourful and step-by-step approach, by using this book you will soon become an expert in making lovely, textured crochet. Find out about hooks and yarns, pattern notation and basic techniques, then follow the instructions and patterns for creating a whole array of bobbles, popcorns and puffs. At the end, there's a selection of projects for you to create, and a handy fold-out flap to use as a reference while you work.

IMAGES
Close-up images with step-by-step instructions.

Start here...

There are patterns for each of the categories of bobbles, popcorns and puffs. Each category is shown first of all as a step-by-step sequence. Practice this before moving onto the patterns.

VIDEO CLIPS
Where you see the phone icon we have put together a video to provide a visual reference to guide you through the process of crocheting a bobble, popcorn or puff. All of the QR codes which link to the videos are on page 96.

One of crochet's distinguishing features is its capacity for texture, and the three techniques of making bobbles, puffs and popcorns are very much a part of this. Understanding how to form and use them will open up a wider field for you. The stitch instructions and tips and tricks dotted throughout are intended to build your confidence by addressing some typical problems and filling in some gaps in understanding.

Bobbles, puffs and popcorns are not just for texture, of course; they are a great vehicle for playing with colours too, and you can create some surprising and delightful effects as you experiment with palettes and practise your skills.

So, I am thrilled to have this opportunity to share my love for this healthful hobby and hope to be able to smooth the pathway for you towards the good feeling it gives me.

Lindy's cat, Tuna, admiring some of her beautiful crochet work. Careful with those claws, Tuna!

LINDY ZUBAIRY Find out more about Lindy at **www.yocrochet.co.uk**

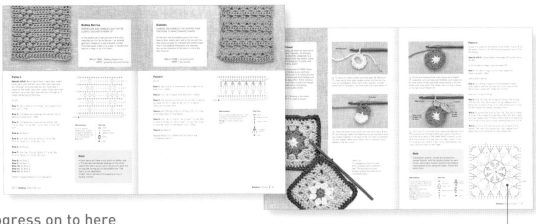

...progress on to here

All patterns come with a written pattern, chart and swatch; complex patterns also have an explanatory step-by-step sequence, showing how-to.

Puff Ball Bag

CHARTS AND KEYS
Charts are colour keyed – each colour change indicates a new round or row. Chart key is shown with each chart.

PROJECTS
Clear written patterns are accompanied by beautiful images of each finished crochet piece.

Chapter 1
The Classroom

Many questions can arise when you embark on a
new skill, so this section is for your reference
and guidance. It's worth reading through before
you start crocheting, to help avoid possible
pitfalls as you practise and provide a firm
foundational knowledge of crochet materials and
tools. You can also dip back in when you need
how-to reminders or troubleshooting clues.

Yarns and Hooks

Selecting the type of yarn and the size of hook you are going to use will have a big impact on the outcome of your piece, as the relationship between yarn weight (thickness) and hook measurement is key.

Choosing yarn and hooks

You can make bobbles, puffs and popcorns with anything that can be wound into a ball. The range of possibilities can be overwhelming. Starting with traditional yarns made from natural fibres such as wool, cotton, linen and silk, as well as synthetic yarns such as acrylic and nylon, and a few thousand combinations in between, there's enough choice to last a lifetime! Any of these can manifest in an equally broad range of colours, twists, textures and weights – from the finest hair threads to the most robust of ropes. Venture away from the yarn shop and you'll continue to encounter suitable materials such as garden twines in natural hemps or indestructible polycarbonates, superfine metal threadwire and leather or suede shoestrings. Discovering and experimenting with all these textures and colours is one

On these pages, the individual crochet circles are shown at 50 per cent of their actual size next to the corresponding hook shown at full size. The same circles are shown at their actual size in the row above.

of the great and endless joys of this craft. Throw yourself in with abandon!

Choosing a hook type is really about how well it supports you to crochet easily and enjoyably. Soft, squishy, ergonomic ones are very comfortable. Wooden and bamboo hooks look attractive and natural. Aluminium hooks are pleasingly weighty and your stitches will glide effortlessly over them. Plastic and gel are lightweight and looks cute. The only way to find your preference is to try out a few.

Hook sizes have been standardised in modern times, but if you are in possession of a set of antique or foreign ones, all is not lost, invest in a size gauge and give them a new lease of life in the 21st century.

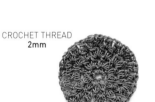

CROCHET THREAD
2mm

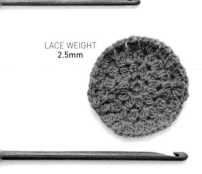

LACE WEIGHT
2.5mm

4-PLY
3mm

DOUBLE KNITTING (DK)
4mm

Matching yarn weights and hooks

Yarn weights are largely fixed but there remains a degree of variation – one manufacturer's 'Aran' is another one's 'chunky'. In addition to this is the fact that no two crocheters work at the same tension (for further information on this, see pages 24–25). Indeed, your own tension may vary according to circumstance.

There is a great deal of room for experimenting here. Generally, you will find that the bigger the hook the more open, airy and draping the final fabric – good for garments. While the smaller the hook compared with the yarn weight, the tighter and stiffer your finished piece will be – good for containers and other household items. With this in mind, you can use the examples on these pages as a general indicator.

**SUPER-CHUNKY
7mm**

**CHUNKY
6mm**

**ARAN
5mm**

Reading Patterns

It's easy to panic or feel impatient when faced with a great wall of 'code and hieroglyphics', as crochet patterns can appear, but reading patterns need not be a stumbling block.

Try reading this out loud:

'Rnd 1: 1ch, 1dc, 1tr, 1dc, 1tr, 1dc, 1tr.'

You should have read:
'Round One: one chain, one double crochet, one treble, one double crochet, one treble, one double crochet, one treble.'

Abbreviations

You'll soon see that these crochet terms are not code, they are simply abbreviations. They are intended to make the instructions take up less sp on the p. Most patterns will provide a quick reference key so that you don't need to memorise anything and you'll find you can work out most of them as you go. For example, *ch* is short for *chain*, *tr* is short for *treble* and *dc* is short for *double crochet*.

Other common abbreviations include: htr (half treble), dtr (double treble), sl st (slip stitch), sk (skip), yo (yarn over) and yrh (yarn round hook).

Some less obvious abbreviations include: 2trtog (two trebles together) – this is a decrease (see full instructions on pages 20–21). There is a little family of these – 3trtog (three trebles together), 2dctog (two double crochets together), 4dtrtog (four double trebles together) and so on.

WS and RS: these are respectively 'wrong side' and 'right side'. Some stitches only look good on one side (the right side). The pattern instructions will keep you on track. See page 94 for a list of common abbreviations used in this book.

Other written instructions

Sometimes you see the term *'counts as first stitch'*. As you begin a new row or round you need to make a turning chain, which hitches you up to the height of the stitch you are about to work. For a row of half trebles, the turning chain will consist of two chains, for a row of trebles it will be three and so on. The turning chain makes a post, which then acts as a stitch in its own right and must be counted as such.

This means you need to call it 'one' when you're counting stitches and you also need to remember it's a stitch when you return to it on the following row and make your last stitch into the top of it.

The turning chain creates a 'post' that counts as the first stitch. To count as a half treble it needs to be 2 chains, a treble needs to be 3 chains and a double treble needs 4 chains.

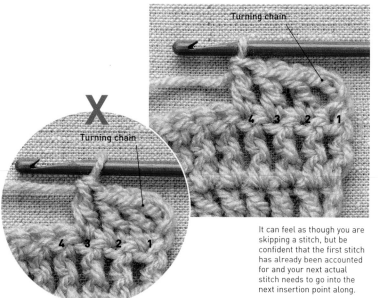

Take care not to make your first 'real' stitch into the base of your turning chain, but one stitch along, or you will find you have increased at the start of your row.

It can feel as though you are skipping a stitch, but be confident that the first stitch has already been accounted for and your next actual stitch needs to go into the next insertion point along.

Stitch 'equations'

To shorten instructions, repeating sequences of stitches are written out in full only the once. You saw earlier the instruction, 'Rnd 1: 1ch, 1dc, 1tr, 1dc, 1tr, 1dc, 1tr'. This is repetitive and easy to get lost in.

A much neater way to show the same instruction would be 'Rnd 1: 1ch, [1dc, 1tr] x 3'. One double crochet followed by one treble is a sequence, so it is written once, then bracketed, and an indication is given at the end of the bracketed section of how many times the sequence must be followed.

Another method of denoting a repeated sequence in a pattern is to use an asterisk. For example: 'Rnd 1: 1ch, *1dc, 1tr, repeat from * x 3'. This is particularly handy in more complex patterns where more than one sequence is repeated in a grander sequence.

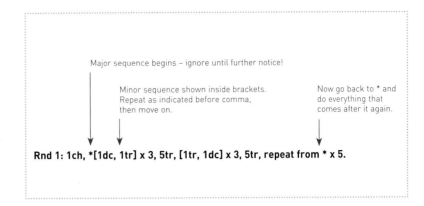

Major sequence begins – ignore until further notice!

Minor sequence shown inside brackets. Repeat as indicated before comma, then move on.

Now go back to * and do everything that comes after it again.

Rnd 1: 1ch, *[1dc, 1tr] x 3, 5tr, [1tr, 1dc] x 3, 5tr, repeat from * x 5.

The asterisk comes into its own when you are asked to 'repeat from *'. Then you go back and start again from that point (see example in box above). Here, we begin with one chain, work the first sequence in brackets three times, work five trebles, then work the second sequence three times followed by five trebles, then go back to where the asterisk appears and begin again at the first sequence, following the instructions through again. Go back to the asterisk three further times before moving on.

Charts

Charts are stylized versions of a real piece of crochet. Read them from the bottom up, as they begin with the foundation and work upwards. For working in the round, read them from the middle outwards, just as you work. Look carefully though – there will be a pointer to tell you where the start is. As with the abbreviated written instructions, there is always a key to a chart.

Charts can clarify complex instructions that are difficult to describe in words. Often they are colour-coded, which can help keep track of rows and rounds. Most chart symbols look much like their real stitch counterparts. For example, the chain looks quite like a chain and the half treble, treble, etc. bear a family resemblance as they do in the way that they are constructed. The double crochet is a little bit different, but not too hard to remember.

Common chart symbols

Here are some of the chart symbols you'll find in this book, along with the name of the stitch and, where applicable, its abbreviation.

Chart symbol	Name of stitch	Abbreviation
	Chain	ch
	Double crochet	dc
	Half treble	htr
	Treble	tr
	Bobble	bbl
	Puff	–
	Popcorn	pc
	3 trebles together	3trtog

Using Patterns and Charts

These pages provide a template for cross-referencing written instructions, charts, keys and photographs that will offer some answers to common questions associated with pattern reading.

A **START** Ch 12.

B **Row 1:** 1dc in 2nd ch from hook, 10dc, turn – 11sts.

C **Row 2:** 3ch (counts as first st), [1bbl, 1ch] x 4, 1bbl, 1tr, turn – 5bbl, 4ch, 2tr including 3ch that counts as first st (11sts).

D **Row 3:** 3ch (counts as first st), 1bbl in sp between tr and bbl in row below, 1ch, [1bbl in 1-ch sp, 1ch] x 4, 1tr in top of 3ch, turn – 5bbl, 5ch, 2tr inc 3ch that counts as first st (12sts).

E **Row 4:** 2ch (counts as first st), [1htr in next 1-ch sp, 1htr in top of next bbl] x 5, turn – 11sts.

F **Row 5:** 2ch (counts as first st), 10htr, turn – 11sts.

G **Row 6:** 3ch (counts as first st), [1puff, 1ch] x 4, 1puff, 1tr, turn – 5puff, 4ch, 2tr inc 3ch that counts as first st (11sts).

H **Row 7:** 1ch (does NOT count as first st), 1dc in tr, [1dc in puff, 1dc in 1-ch sp] x 4, 1dc in puff, 1dc in top of 3-ch – 11sts.

I **Row 8:** 2ch (counts as first st) 10htr, turn – 11sts.

J **Row 9:** 3tr (counts as first st), 2tr, 1pc, 3tr, 1pc, 3tr, turn – 9tr inc 3ch that counts as first st (11sts).

K **Row 10:** 2ch (counts as first st), 1htr in each of next 2tr, 1htr in next pc, 1htr in each of next 3tr, 1htr in next pc, 1htr in each of last 2tr, 1htr in top of 3ch, turn – 11sts.

L **Row 11:** 1ch (does NOT count as first st), 11dc, turn – 11sts.

M **Row 12:** 1bry in first dc, [1 sl st in next dc, 1bry in next dc] x 5, turn – 6bry, 5sl st (11sts).

N **Row 13:** 1ch (does NOT count as first st), 1dc in first bry, [1dc in next sl st, 1dc in next bry] x 5, turn – 11sts.

O **Row 14:** 1sl st in first dc, [1bry in next dc, 1sl st in next dc] x 5, turn – 5 bry, 6sl st (11sts).

P **Row 15:** 1ch (does NOT count as first st), 1dc in first bry, [1dc in next sl st, 1dc in next bry] x 5, turn – 11sts.

Q **Row 16:** As Row 12.

R **Row 17:** As Row 13.

S **Row 18:** 4ch (counts as first st), 10dtr, turn – 11sts.

T **Row 19:** 3ch (counts as first st), [1tbob, 3trtog] x 3, 1tbob, 1tr into 4ch, turn – 4tbob, 3 x 3trtog, 2tr inc 3ch that counts as first st.

U **Row 20:** 3ch (counts as first st), [sk tbob, 3tr in top of 3trtog] x 3, sk tbob, 1tr in top of 3ch, turn – 11sts inc 3ch that counts as first st.

V **Row 21:** 1ch (does NOT count as first st), 1dc in first tr, 10dc, turn – 11sts.

W **Row 22:** 1ch (does NOT count as first st), 1dc in first dc, 10dc, turn – 11sts.

X **Row 23:** 2ch (counts as first st), 1htr, [1pb, 2htr] x 3, turn – 3pb, 8htr inc 2ch that counts as first st.

Y **Row 24:** 1ch (does NOT count as first st), [1dc in each of next 2 htr, 1dc in top of pb] x 3, 1dc in last htr, 1dc in top of 2-ch, fasten off.

ABBREVIATION KEY
The following abbreviations relate to the special stitches used in the sample. For a list of common abbreviations see page 94.
bry = berry
pb = puff ball
bbl = 4-post bobble
pc = 4-post popcorn
3trtog = 3 trebles together (decrease)
tbob = travelling bobble

CHART KEY

⬭	chain
•	slip stitch
+	double crochet
T	half treble crochet
↑	treble crochet
⯅	double treble crochet
berry symbol	berry
puff ball symbol	puff ball
4-post bobble symbol	4-post bobble
puff symbol	puff
4-post popcorn symbol	4-post popcorn
3 trebles together symbol	3 trebles together (decrease)
travelling bobble symbol	travelling bobble
▶	start

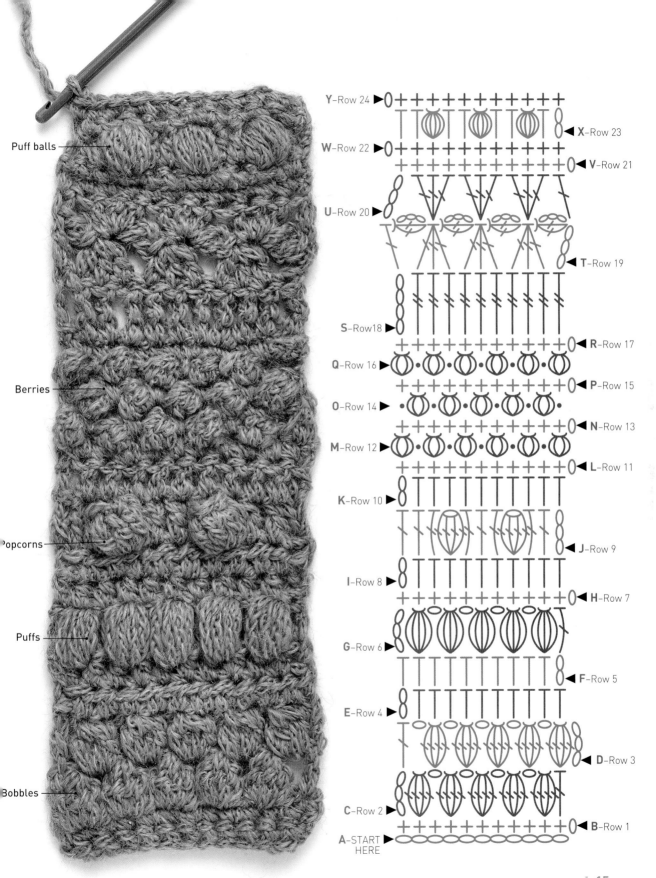

Puff balls

Berries

Popcorns

Puffs

Bobbles

Y–Row 24
X–Row 23
W–Row 22
V–Row 21
U–Row 20
T–Row 19
S–Row18
R–Row 17
Q–Row 16
P–Row 15
O–Row 14
N–Row 13
M–Row 12
L–Row 11
K–Row 10
J–Row 9
I–Row 8
H–Row 7
G–Row 6
F–Row 5
E–Row 4
D–Row 3
C–Row 2
B–Row 1
A–START HERE

— Slip Stitch

•

— Double crochet

+

— Half Treble

T

— Treble

F

— Double treble

F

Basic Techniques

As this book is focussed on creating bobbles, popcorns and puffs, you will probably already have a little experience with simpler forms of crochet. However, we've included a refresher course here on the basic techniques for your convenience.

Basic Stitches

Here, you'll find a reminder of the basic crochet stitches you'll need.
To practise, make a slip knot on your hook and work a few chains.

SLIP STITCH

This is good for joining the last stitch to the first stitch in rounds and for travelling along a row without making any height in order to reposition without fastening off.

Insert hook, yarn over and pull through both loops on the hook. Here a slip stitch is used to join the last stitch to the first of a round on a circular motif.

Here, a row of slip stitches in a contrasting colour finishes off a swatch (see left).

DOUBLE CROCHET

This is a pretty, usually quite dense, stitch (unless you use a bigger hook than is recommended on the yarn label – can be quite effective). Has ONE turning chain which DOES NOT act as the first stitch.

1 Insert hook, yarn over and pull through, leaving two loops on the hook.

2 Yarn over a second time and pull through both loops.

HALF TREBLE

The half treble creates an interim height between the shorter double crochet and the taller treble – useful in shaping flower petals. Straight treble stitching forms distinct horizontal ridges in the fabric. The looser you work, the easier it is to pull through all three loops in one go. The turning chain has two chains and is counted as the first stitch.

TREBLE

Straight rows of trebles resemble a row of posts, or a ladder lying on its side. This is arguably the commonest crochet stitch of all. The turning chain has three chains, and is usually counted as the first stitch.

DOUBLE TREBLE

This is a very tall stitch and has even more of a 'ladder' effect than the treble. Predictably, the turning chain has four chains and counts as a stitch. You can continue making taller and taller stitches simply by taking the yarn round the hook more times before you insert it at the beginning of the stitch.

1 Yarn over first, insert hook.

1 Yarn over first, insert hook, yarn over a second time and pull through, leaving three loops on the hook.

1 Yarn round the hook twice, insert hook, yarn over and pull through, leaving four loops on the hook.

2 Yarn over a second time and pull through, leaving three loops on the hook.

2 Yarn over a third time and pull through two loops, leaving two loops on the hook.

2 Yarn over again and pull through two loops, leaving three loops on the hook.

3 Yarn over once more and pull through all three loops.

3 Then yarn over one more time and pull through the remaining two loops.

3 Yarn over again and pull through two loops, leaving two loops on the hook. Yarn over one last time and pull through the remaining two loops.

Working in the Round

One of the things that set crochet apart from knitting is the ease with which you can go round in circles. 'Working in the round' means starting at the centre and working outwards, and it is not restricted to the creation of round items. Indeed, the most iconic of all crochet motifs – the Granny Square – is worked in the round. Choose any of the following three methods to begin.

A RING OF CHAINS
Make a series of chains, perhaps three or five, then join the last one to the first, using a slip stitch.

The centre of this motif may well have a hole using this method, which might be fine. Some 'hairy' yarns, or the use of a smaller than recommended hook might serve to close up the hole.

WORKING INTO THE SECOND CHAIN
Start by working just two chains, and then using the second chain from the hook as your centre hole, in which to work all the stitches of Round One.

This may seem an impossibly small space in which to work so many stitches, but, generally speaking, you'll find the chain is able to expand to accommodate as many stitches as you need. Indeed, you still might get a hole in the middle as it will not tighten again once it has expanded.

MAGIC (DRAWSTRING) RING

1 Wind some yarn around your finger a couple of times, then carefully remove your finger, holding the ring of yarn to stop it from disintegrating. Insert your hook through the middle of the ring and hold the yarn in place against the hook with your forefinger.

2 Yarn over and gently pull through the ring, keeping the new loop small on the hook, yarn over again, pull through the small loop on the hook and then tighten the ring. You will have one tight loop on the hook, and a reasonably secure but much larger ring hanging below.

3 Your first round of stitches is worked into this ring and joined into a full circle with a slip stitch.

4 Now you are ready to draw the magic ring closed. Resting your work in your upturned palm, position it so that the tail attached to the ring is hanging down between your fingers, then pull it firmly until the ring closes up in your hand.

Changing Colour and Joining in New Yarn

When joining in new yarn, whether it is because you have used up a ball or you wish to change colour, the method is the same. It is possible to join a new yarn at the edge of the work or in the middle. Either way, the point at which the swap occurs is as you make the last yarn-over of the stitch before the new colour begins.

Note

Some of the colourwork swatches in this book (see page 42) use non-standard colour change techniques because they are not standard stitches. Be sure to read the patterns carefully. Each is provided with full instructions.

1 In the middle of the row, drape the new colour over the hook, with the short end at the back.

2 Pinch the yarn-over ends together as you pull it through the loops. No need to secure at this point.

3 You might choose to work the short end into the first few stitches after the colour change in order to avoid having to weave it in later. To do this, lay it along the top of the row ahead.

WHEN (AND WHEN NOT) TO FASTEN OFF

For two- or three-colour stripe schemes with edges that will have a border or a seam, don't fasten off the old colour – leave it to trail up the sides and be worked in again later. Create stripes in even row numbers so that the working yarn is on the correct edge when you want it again. This will cut down considerably on the 'weaving in' of ends.

At the end of the row, the principle is generally the same as for changing colour in the middle; it is still done in the last yarn-over of the stitch before.

When making shapes or pictures with colour, you will need to be decisive about which is the right side (front) and which is the wrong side (back or reverse) because colour changes usually look smarter on one side than the other.

Right side

Wrong side

Increasing and Decreasing

Shaping your piece of crochet can be achieved by increasing or decreasing the number of stitches in a row.

INCREASING BY SMALL AMOUNTS

The simplest method of increasing is to work more than one stitch into the same base. A pattern instruction for this might be, '2tr in next st' (two trebles in next stitch). Here, two trebles are worked into the same place on each end of every row, creating a marked increase row on row.

To increase bobbles, puffs and popcorns, you can simply work more than one into the same stitch in a similar fashion.

For patterns containing a mixture of standard stitches and textural motifs, increase subtly using the standard stitches, or make a design feature of an increase in bobbles, puffs or popcorns.

INCREASING BY LARGE AMOUNTS

Greater increases can be achieved simply by repeating the above method evenly across the row. This creates a curved edge. If you want to create a more dramatic increase, such as an 'L' or 'T' shape, you will need to add several stitches at the edge.

1 Work a number of extra chains at the end of the row.

2 Turn and work back along the chains as on any foundation row, continuing onwards at the main body of work.

Try this!

You get a neater raw edge on foundation chains if you work into the back bumps of the chains (see page 57 for more explanation of back bumps).

3 To increase the same amount on the other edge, stop short of the end of the same row and, using a new length of the same yarn, attach it at the end of the row and work a corresponding number of chains.

4 Picking up your original stitching, continue on to the end of the row and into the new chain, turning at the end as normal.

DECREASING BY SMALL AMOUNTS

You can decrease by skipping stitches, especially on rows of double crochet, but with taller and more complex stitches this tends to create noticeable holes. You'll get a better finish by using a cluster method, which involves working stitches together. In the example below, three stitches are turned into one. In a pattern this might be called 'three trebles together' abbreviated as 3trtog. You also might see 3dctog, or 3dtrtog, depending on which stitch is being worked. For a smaller decrease you would work two trebles together (2trtog).

HOW TO FORM A CLUSTER DECREASE

1 Work one stitch through as normal until you reach the last yarn-over and then stop short with two loops left on the hook.

2 Begin a new stitch in the next stitch along, working through the entire stitch but stopping short of the final yarn-over, leaving three loops on the hook.

3 Begin another stitch in the next place along, and pull through all four loops on the hook on the last yarn-over.

DECREASING BY LARGER AMOUNTS

You can create a larger decrease by cluster-decreasing evenly and repeatedly along the row. If you want to create a sudden corner at the edge, you use slip stitches. This is an easier method for making sleeves in an already complex stitch pattern and is often used in loose-fitting or baby garments.

1 Work to the end of the last wide row, turn and slip stitch the number of stitches you intend to 'lose' (slip stitches create almost no height and are good for repositioning yourself without fastening off).

2 At the other end of the decrease row, stop short of the edge by the same number of stitches lost at the other edge.

What are Bobbles, Puffs and Popcorns?

Bobbles, popcorns and puffs are motifs that appear throughout crochet from its earliest beginnings and, as such, are part of a core skill set. In repeat patterns or artfully positioned for maximum impact on an expanse of smoother stitching, purely for texture or combined with clever colouring, these charming features make it easy for anyone wishing to add interest and character to their crafting.

What is the difference between the three?

Crochet is a relatively young craft and its lexicon continues to evolve. The terms used here are reasonably common in written crochet design today. The common feature across all three is that each one occupies only the space of a single stitch in the pattern.

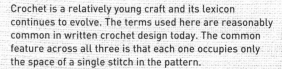

3-post Bobble

Three distinct posts can be identified, each arising from the same base and closed together at the top.

THE BOBBLE

A basic bobble is a group of uncompleted treble stitches that are worked into the same spot at their base, and then finished all together into one stitch at the top. There can be any number of incomplete trebles; the more there are, the bigger the bump, because they only ever take up the space of a single stitch. The pattern created by a series of bobbles is notable as much for the gaps between them as it is for the tubby silhouettes of the bobbles themselves.

THE POPCORN

A popcorn is different because it is made from multiple complete trebles. These, like the bobble, are all worked into the same space (or stitch) at the base, and drawn into one stitch at the top. But because they are finished stitches in their own right before they are pulled together, the stitch posts are longer and they make one seriously three-dimensional bump. The hollow ball that emerges by this technique has a flat top like a teacup.

Standard 5-post popcorn

Popcorns tend to have a round belly and a flat top. As with the bobble, each post arises from the same base but only two of them are actually adjoined at the top – the first and the last – leaving the other stitches freedom to stand out more.

THE PUFF

This yarn-gobbling nubble is the maverick of the three as it doesn't use trebles at all. Appearing quite smooth and cushioned, it is a solid mass of long threads. Again working into the same base, it is made by pulling up multiple long loops that are about as tall as a treble stitch, usually about 10 of them in any one puff, and then drawing them all together at the top.

5-pass puff

Puffs resemble embroidery satin stitches with their long strands, unbroken by knots or twists. Each 'pass' (or insertion) involves two yarn-overs and therefore creates two loops, so a 5-pass puff will have 10 loops, plus the one that was already on the hook at the start.

Getting the Size Right

'Tension' in crochet is the word used to describe the number of stitches and rows in a given measurement (e.g. 15 stitches to 10 cm or 5 rows to 10 cm). Stitch and row counts can, however, sometimes bear little resemblance to a finished piece due to differences in personal crochet styles, stress levels, the yarn in use and even the time of day it is made.

For anything that needs to fit, getting the tension to match the pattern is fairly important. If you can use the exact same yarn and hook size as advised, this will be a good start but you will still need to work up a reasonably generous-sized swatch before you begin. Try making a square with around 20 stitches to the row (this equates to 10 bobbles on a standard bricked bobble – see page 32 – format, for example). Then block the swatch (see page 27 Finishing Your Work) before measuring the stitch and row counts using a ruler.

- If you have fewer stitches and rows to the given measure, your hook is too big. You can remedy this by using a smaller hook size.
- If you have too many stitches and rows to the given measure, your hook is too small; select one the next size up and swatch again.

Try this!

You may note that your foundation chain is very tight in comparison with the swatch overall. If so, try using a larger hook on the chain and then swapping down for the main body of the crocheting.

BOBBLES – 2.5MM HOOK

9 rows to 10cm

21 stitches to 10cm

BOBBLES – 4MM HOOK

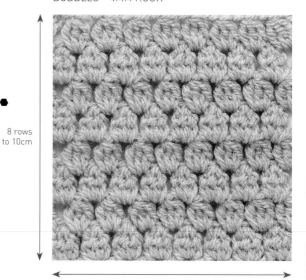

8 rows to 10cm

18 stitches to 10cm

All in Double Knit Weight Yarn.

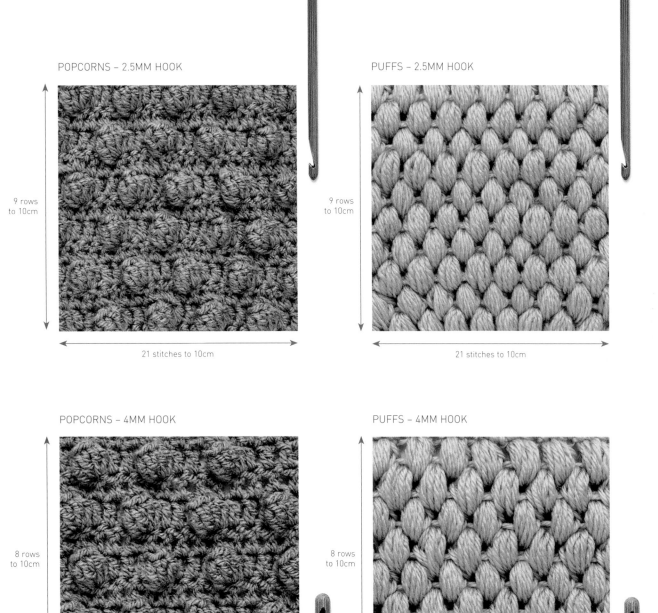

POPCORNS – 2.5MM HOOK

9 rows to 10cm

21 stitches to 10cm

PUFFS – 2.5MM HOOK

9 rows to 10cm

21 stitches to 10cm

POPCORNS – 4MM HOOK

8 rows to 10cm

18 stitches to 10cm

PUFFS – 4MM HOOK

8 rows to 10cm

18 stitches to 10cm

Finishing Your Work

Giving your crochet a proper finish can make a world of difference to your project. This section covers some common techniques to give your work a professional look: blocking to even out and set the shape; weaving in any loose threads; and joining individual pieces together.

Keeping notes

A notebook for recording all your crochet details as you go along is such a good idea. You think you're going to remember which yarn it was, where you bought it, how many balls or skeins you used, which pattern book contained the stitch, or how you adapted it, but you often won't! Jot it all down as you go. This is even more essential if you tend to go off pattern, use alternative yarns, do your own designing and/or write patterns for others.

Labelling swatches

Creating tension swatches (see pages 24–25) is excellent practice, as is making squares just to try out interesting new stitches. You can buy tiny labels in stationers, complete with little strings. Just scribble the yarn name and the hook size on one, tie it onto a corner of the swatch and tuck it away somewhere out of the light so it doesn't fade (ideally joined by a lavender bag to keep the moths at bay).

Recording yarn information

All the information about the yarn, including the washing instructions, is held on the ball band (the paper sleeve on the ball or skein). The quickest method to keep a record of this is to snip off a short length of the yarn before you do anything else and tie it round the ball band. In this way the information is paired up with the yarn itself. You could glue this in your notebook, keep it in a card referencing system, or pop it in a tin, it's up to you, but it is certainly worth the extra effort to avoid a lot of frustration later.

Blocking

If your swatches are wonky or curl up at the edges, don't worry because steam blocking can be nothing short of miraculous. This is how crocheted items look so good in the pictures – you should have seen them before they were blocked!

1 Pin your piece of crochet to an ironing board using many large, bead-headed pins, forming it into the shape and size you want it to be (the more out of shape your swatch, the more pins you'll need). Angle the pins away from the centre. Use a ruler, template or set square to get the shape right and be very precise – the more care you take at this point, the better the result.

2 Fill up a steam iron with water and switch on the steam setting. Never touch the crochet with the iron, as you don't want to flatten out all the lovely, three-dimensional texture, particularly with bobbles, puffs and popcorns. Instead, hovering over the swatch, press the steam booster button until your handiwork has been well and truly drenched in the hot cloud of steam. Leave the piece on the board until it is completely dry. You'll find when you take out the pins that it has submitted to your will!

Weaving in ends

Ends may be worked into the back of the work using a crochet hook to pull through strands in as haphazard a number of directions as possible (running it under strands in a straight line makes it too easy to undo). Your optimum length of yarn for weaving in is around 5cm. If you have at least 10cm tail left, you can thread the end onto a blunt-ended needle and stitch it under strands on the reverse side in a similar fashion. You can then cut it off once you have worked in around 5cm. Weaving in ends can be quite a boring process, so two ways to avoid it are described here.

WEAVING IN AS YOU GO ALONG
When joining in a new yarn or colour, work the short end (or tail) into the next few stitches by laying it over the top of them and crocheting round it. This is easier when working standard stitches rather than bobbles, puffs or popcorns, but not impossible with these textured stitches. You can make life even easier for yourself by using the hook to pull the tail through the first few stitches first, which keeps it completely under control.

LEAVING IT HANGING UNTIL NEEDED AGAIN
If you are going to use the same colour again later in a series of stripes, don't fasten off, just trail it up the side until it is required again. This works only with even numbers of rows, leaving the trailing yarn on the same edge where it will be required later. It also makes sense only if the edge will be hidden in a seam or under a border or finishing edge.

Joining

There are two approaches to joining pieces. You can stitch together blocks and seams with a blunt-ended needle or you can crochet them. Either way, use the same yarn as the crocheted piece. If the two pieces are in different colours, select one of them. If the yarn is particularly textured or bulky, try to find one in a blending colour that is a bit finer so that it will easily pass through the eye of your needle and keep the bulk down.

IMPORTANT TIPS

• When making pieces with bobbles, puffs or popcorns for joining, it is advisable to start and end each row with a standard treble or half treble stitch (whatever fits with the particular stitch pattern), so that you have something clear to work around when joining the side edges.

• Steam block (see page 27) each piece before joining – this makes it much easier to match them evenly.

• Joining the top and bottom of a crocheted block is easier as you can work straight into each stitch, matching each corresponding one to the other piece, whereas down the sides is a little less clear. As a rule of thumb: into the side of a double crochet row, work one stitch and in treble rows work two. Use your discretion, but take particular care to join up the correct corresponding rows and match stripes precisely. If you have too many stitches your seam will begin to spread out and frill. If not enough, it will gather and pucker. Pin first to be sure.

SEWING

There are many stitches you can use when sewing the join. Here are two standard stitches you can use: backstitch and chain stitch.

Back stitch: pin pieces right sides together and using a blunt-ended needle, backstitch evenly, just in from the edge. Fasten off securely, as this method can unravel easily. It creates a firm, invisible seam on the right side but can be bulky.

Chain stitch: pin pieces right sides together and using a blunt-ended needle, chain stitch evenly, just in from the edge. It creates a strong, firm, invisible seam on the right side but can be bulky.

Two tools for joining – the hook and the blunt-ended needle.

CROCHETING

There are many stitches you can use when crocheting the join. Here are examples of some common methods. First, a double crochet worked through both pieces at the same time (**A**). This method, if worked on the 'wrong' side, will create a hidden seam (**B**), but if on the right side can be a design feature as it creates a ridge (**C**). You can emphasise this further by using a contrasting colour.

You can also create a wide, flat joining band by zigzagging between the pieces with a double crochet stitch in one piece at a time, interspersed with chains (**D**). This becomes a prominent design feature. Be aware that this will add substantially to the finished size of an item made of multiple blocks.

When joining multiple blocks in a patchwork configuration, start by creating strips of joined pieces, steam block the strips and join them together in long seams. (**E**). Usually the entire patchwork is enclosed in a border to finish.

A–Double crochet worked through both pieces: pin pieces right sides together and, using a crochet hook the same size as for the original pieces, work a row of double crochet into the edges of both pieces at the same time.

B–Double crochet worked on the WS: steam block your seam to make it crisp and flat on the right side, as shown. There will still be a ridge on the reverse side.

C–Double crochet worked on the RS: here the ridge becomes a design feature.

D–Double crochet zigzag seam: a lacy zigzag effect is created by working double crochets into one piece at a time, making one chain in between each and skipping alternate stitches.

E–Making strips of blocks and joining in long seams: once you have created two strips of joined squares, you can then join thpse strips in a long, unbroken seam of whichever method you have adopted.

Chapter 2
The Techniques

Bobbles, popcorns and puffs are versatile crochet components, so here you'll find instructions for the most basic and traditional patterns at the beginning of each section. Practising these with a variety of yarns and hooks will yield plenty of design inspiration. When you are ready, you can move on to the surprising variations on these techniques that I've included to really open up the field.

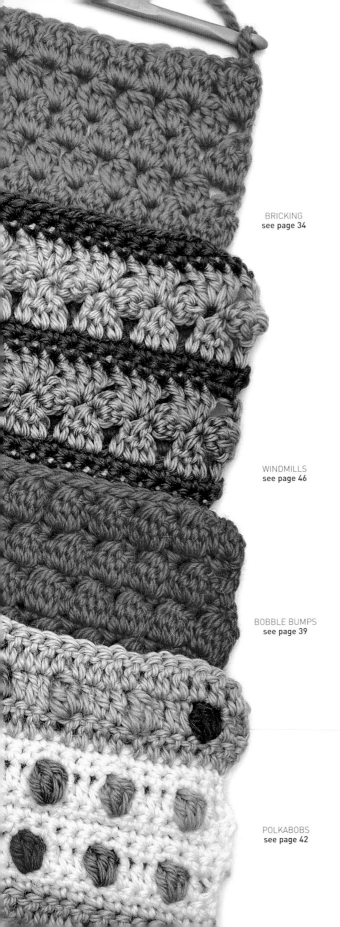

BRICKING
see page 34

WINDMILLS
see page 46

BOBBLE BUMPS
see page 39

POLKABOBS
see page 42

Bobbles

A bobble is a group of stitches (usually trebles) worked unfinished into the same place at the base, and joined together with a single yarn-over at the top. A three-post bobble is quite flat and subtle, its texture more visual than tactile; but add more posts and you get something altogether chubbier and more three-dimensional. This makes it the most versatile of the three, appearing across the craft, from delicate Irish lacework through to super-chunky homewares, accessories and garments. Slightly less demanding than popcorns or puffs, bobbles are an essential part of the crocheter's skill set, opening up multiple new avenues for crochet exploration.

3-post bobble

BOBBLES CAN HAVE ANY NUMBER OF 'POSTS'. THE MORE THEY HAVE, THE MORE 3D THEY ARE. HERE, A STANDARD 3-POST BOBBLE IS BEING WORKED INTO A FOUNDATION ROW OF DOUBLE CROCHET STITCHES (SEE 'BRICKING STITCH', PAGE 34).

Video clip

Watch the video clip for working a 3-post bobble (see page 33). This helpful visual reference will guide you through the process. To link to the video, use your mobile phone to scan the QR code on page 96.

Working a standard 3-post bobble

1 In the place indicated in the pattern, begin to create a treble stitch (i.e.: yarn over, insert hook, yarn over and pull through, yarn over again and pull through two loops). **Stop before the treble stitch is complete**, leaving two loops on the hook.

2 Begin a second treble in the same place as the first, and stop again before you work the last yarn-over (i.e.: yarn over, insert hook, yarn over and pull through, yarn over and pull through two loops, then stop, leaving three loops on the hook.)

3 Begin a third treble in the same place as the first two, again stopping short of the last yarn-over. You should now have three posts in the same place and four loops on the hook. (The fourth loop is left over from your previous stitch, which here is the turning chain).

4 Yarn over and pull through all four loops on the hook, leaving you with one loop. Ta *dah* – you have created a three-post bobble!

5 Make one more chain, which will seem to draw the bobble into shape. This is actually an 'in-between' chain that creates a small space between this and the next bobble.

6 On subsequent rows each bobble is often worked into the one-chain space between two bobbles in the row below (see Bricking swatch, page 34).

Bricking

THIS LAYOUT, WITH BOBBLES BETWEEN
BOBBLES – EACH ROW CONSTRUCTED
OFFSET LIKE BRICKWORK – IS AN OLD
FAVOURITE.

Once you get past the foundation row and
begin to work bobbles between bobbles,
you'll soon fall into a relaxing rhythm. This
technique may be used to make a wide
range of snuggly items, from scarves,
cowls and mitts, to beanies, bobble hats
and baby blankets.

SKILLS TAKE | Working multiple stitches
AWAY | into one place

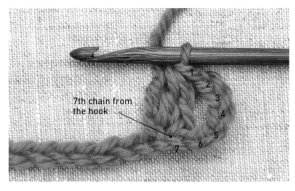

7th chain from
the hook

1 Make a foundation chain as required in the pattern (in our
instructions, opposite, 25 chains). Row 1: work a 3-post
bobble into the 7th chain from the hook (see Steps 1–4 for
standard 3-post bobble on page 33).

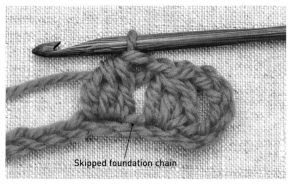

Skipped foundation chain

2 Chain 1 (this both creates a gap between this and the
next bobble and finishes the bobble shape). Skipping the
next foundation chain, work another 3-post bobble into the
following chain. Continue working one bobble, one chain,
skipping a foundation chain in between each.

VARIATION
Try changing colour on each row
(see page 19). The two-colour row
is achieved by working two strands
of colour as one. The yarn ends are
hidden inside a row of double crochet
down each side.

Treble worked into last chain

3 Work along the row until you have two chains left. Skip the first of these and work a treble stitch (not a whole bobble) into the last chain. Turn the work. Your row of bobbles separated by single chains has a 'post' at each end.

4 For next, and all subsequent rows, make 3 chains to start (the turning chain acts as a treble stitch) and then follow the 'one-chain, one bobble' sequence all along the row, **working each bobble into the one-chain spaces between the bobbles**. At the end of the row work a treble into the top of the turning chain. Pay careful attention to the chart showing the minor differences between rows 2 and 3, which are then repeated in sequence.

Try this!

Make a scarf in only 8 rows, with a starting chain of 300 to make 150 bobbles per row for a neat, long edge; hide the short edges under a fringe.

Pattern

Now have a look at how this looks written in proper pattern instruction notation. Note the convention of the 'special stitch'. Generally the assumption is that you know the standard stitches – double crochet, treble, etc. – as described in 'Basic Stitches', pages 16–17.

Special stitch: 3-post bobble (see page 33), written here as 'bbl'.

Ch 25 (multiple of 2 + 5)

Row 1: 1bbl in 7th ch from hook (turning chain counts as a tr, plus 1ch), (1ch, sk 1ch, 1 bbl in next ch) x 8, 1ch, sk 1ch, 1tr in last ch, turn – 9 bbl, 10 1-ch sps and 2 tr.

Row 2: 3ch, 1bbl in 1-ch sp between tr and next bobble in row below, (1ch, 1 bbl in next 1-ch sp) x 9, 1tr in last st – 10 bbl, 2 tr, 8 1-ch sps.

Row 3: 4ch (turning chain counts as first st, plus 1ch), [1bbl in next 1-ch sp, 1ch] x 9, 1ch, 1tr in top of turning chain of row below.

Repeat rows 2 and 3 in sequence.

Abbreviations

A list of common abbreviations is given on page 94. Below are some special ones used in this stitch pattern.
bbl = 3-post bobble (see 'Special stitch')
1-ch sp = space created by one chain

Chart key

○ chain

T treble

⬥ 3-post bobble

▶ start

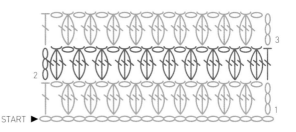

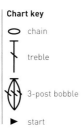

START ▶

Granny Flower

THE RECTANGULAR PART OF THIS MOTIF IS A STANDARD 'GRANNY' OR AFGHAN SQUARE. THE CENTRE, HOWEVER, IS A BIT OF A BREAK FROM THE NORM, USING EIGHT 3-POST BOBBLES TO LOOK LIKE THE PETALS OF A DAISY.

Each petal is separated by THREE chains that become invisible as you work your next (standard cluster) row. Using only one colour for the traditional stitch background enhances the daisy effect. Either continue making rows of treble clusters for a larger square or finish with a contrasting-coloured row of double crochet.

SKILLS TAKE AWAY | Working in the round to create a square

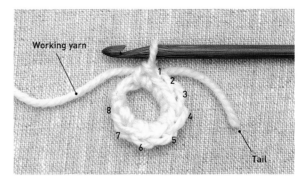

Working yarn

Tail

1 In Colour A, make a magic ring (see page 18). Work one chain stitch, then eight double crochet stitches into the ring, not overlapping. Slide them closer together to make more room if necessary. Join with a slip stitch and fasten off.

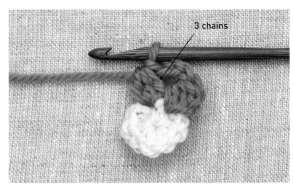

3 chains

2 Insert the hook in any stitch, yarn over with colour B and pull through. Make two chains (counts as first post), work two trebles together in the base of the two-chain to complete the first bobble. Work three chains, then a standard 3-post bobble in the next stitch.

VARIATION
Try swapping Colours A and B for a flower with a different feel. The background and border remain the same for a consistent style.

3 Continue by making three more chains and a bobble repeatedly until you have eight bobbles, each separated by three chains. Finish with three chains joined to the first bobble with a slip stitch. The 'wheel' will turn into a 'flower' on the next round! Fasten off.

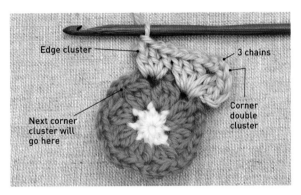

Edge cluster

Next corner cluster will go here

3 chains

Corner double cluster

4 Join Colour C in any three-chain-space and make two chains (counts as the first stitch). Work two trebles, three chains and three more trebles in THE SAME SPACE (creates a corner). Work three trebles in the next space (an 'edge' cluster). Finish the round with two clusters in each corner separated by three chains, and one cluster on each edge.

Note

Subsequent 'granny' rounds are worked in a similar fashion, with the double cluster for each corner, and single clusters worked into however many spaces occur along the edges. Follow the stitch chart.

Abbreviations

A list of common abbreviations is given on page 94. Below are some special ones used in this stitch pattern.
bbl = 3-post bobble (see 'Special stitch')
3-ch sp = three-chain space (space created by three chains)
2trtog = two trebles together (see page 21)

Chart key

○ chain
• slip stitch
◎ magic ring
+ double crochet
† treble

⊕ 3-post bobble
⊼ 2trtog
▶ start

Pattern

Colour A is used for the centre of the flower, Colour B for the petals, Colour C for the background and Colour D for the edging.

Special stitch: 3-post bobble (see page 33), written here as 'bbl'.

In Col A make a magic ring (see page 18).

Rnd 1: 1ch, 8dc in ring, sl st to close, fasten off, draw ring tight – 8sts.

Join Col B in any st.

Rnd 2: 2ch, 2trtog in base of ch (first bobble made), (3ch, 1bbl) in each dc around, 3ch, sl st in top of first bbl to close, fasten off – 8 bbl, 8 x 3-ch sp.

Join Col C in any 3-ch sp.

Rnd 3: (3ch, 2tr, 3ch, 3tr) in same 3-ch sp, *3tr in next 3-ch sp, (3tr, 3ch, 3tr) in next 3-ch sp, repeat from * 3 times, 3tr in next 3-ch sp, sl st in top of first 3ch to close. Do NOT fasten off unless changing colour.

Rnd 4: Sl st into first 3-ch sp, (3ch, 2tr, 3ch, 3tr) in same 3-ch sp, *(3tr in next 3-ch sp) twice, (3tr, 3ch, 3tr) in next 3-ch sp, repeat from * 3 times, (3tr in next 3-ch sp) twice, sl st in top of first 3ch to close, working final yo in Col A.

Rnd 5: In Col A, 1ch, 1dc into sl st, 1dc in each of 2 tr below, *5dc into 3-ch (corner) sp, 12dc, repeat from * twice, 9dc, sl st in first dc to close, fasten off.

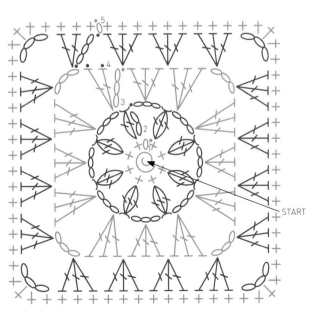

START

Bobdala

USING 3-POST BOBBLES (SEE PAGE 33), THIS SWATCH IS WORKED IN THE ROUND FROM THE CENTRE, JUST LIKE THE GRANNY FLOWER (SEE PAGE 36).

It's called a bobdala in homage to the 'mandala', which is the new name for round crochet shapes that we used to call doilies!

SKILLS TAKE AWAY | Working in the round to make a flat disc

Pattern

Special stitches:

3-post bobble (see page 33), written here as 'bbl'.
3-chain picot (pct) – 3 chains, slip stitch to first chain.

In Col A, make a magic ring (see page 18).

Rnd 1: 3ch, 2trtog into ring (first bobble complete), (3ch, 1 bbl) x 5, 3ch, join to top of 2ch with a sl st, fasten off – 6 bobbles.

Join Col B in any 3-ch space.

Rnd 2: 2ch, 2trtog in base of chain (first bobble complete), 3ch, 1 bbl in same sp as first bbl, (3ch, 1bbl, 3ch, 1bbl in next 3-ch sp) x 5, 3ch, join to top of first 2ch with a sl st, fasten off – 12 bobbles.

Join Col C in any 3-ch sp.

Rnd 3: 2ch, 2trtog in base of chain (first bobble complete), 3ch, 1 bbl in same sp as first bbl, *(3ch, 1bbl in next 3-ch sp), (3ch, 1bbl, 3ch, 1bbl in next 3-ch sp), repeat from * x 4, 3ch, 1bbl in next 3-ch sp, 3ch, join to top of 2-ch with a sl st to close, fasten off – 18 bobbles.

Rejoin Col A in any 3-ch sp.

Rnd 4: 1ch, 2dc, 1pct (2dc, 1pct) in each 3-ch sp around, sl st in first 1ch to close, fasten off.

START

Abbreviations

A list of common abbreviations is given on page 94. Below are some special ones used in this stitch pattern.
bbl = 3-post bobble (see 'Special stitch')
pct = 3-chain picot (see 'Special stitch')
3-ch sp = space created by 3 chains
2trtog = two trebles together (see page 21)

Chart key

⬭ chain
• slip stitch
🌀 magic ring
+ double crochet
2trtog

3-post bobble
3-chain picot
► start

Tips

Note carefully which spaces contain two bobbles and which contain only one. The final round is a quick lesson in making a picot edge.

Bobble Bumps

THESE BOBBLES HAVE HALF TREBLE STITCHES
RATHER THAN CHAIN SPACES BETWEEN THEM,
AND EACH BOBBLE HAS FOUR POSTS.
BETWEEN EACH BOBBLE ROW IS A SPACER
ROW OF DOUBLE CROCHET.

These small differences change the character of
the finished fabric, creating a one-sided pattern
and giving it a more three-dimensional texture.

SKILLS TAKE | Using spacer rows to create a
AWAY | one-sided fabric

Pattern

Special stitch: 4-post bobble (as 3-post bobble
described on page 33 but with a 4th unfinished
treble before completion), written in this
pattern instruction as 'bbl'.

Ch 20.

Row 1: 1dc in 2nd ch from hook, 1dc in each
ch to end – 19sts

Row 2: 2ch, [1bbl in next st, 1htr in next st] x 9,
turn – 9 bobbles and 10 htr (inc turning chain).

Row 3: 1ch, 1dc in each st to end, turn – 19sts.

Row 4: 2ch (counts as first htr), [1 htr in next
st, 1bbl in next st] x 8, 1htr in each of last 2
sts, turn – 8 bobbles and 11 htr inc turning ch.

Row 5: As Row 3.

Repeat Rows 2–5 as required.

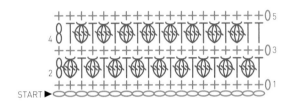

START ▶

Abbreviations

A list of common abbreviations is given
on page 94. Below are some special
ones used in this stitch pattern.
bbl = 4-post bobble (see 'Special stitch')

Chart key

⬭ chain
+ double crochet
T half treble
🪢 4-post bobble
▶ start

Bobble Berries

BERRIES ARE BABY BOBBLES AND THEY'RE SLIGHTLY QUICKER TO WORK UP.

In this swatch, you'll see just one of the many ways that you can lay out berries – as isolated geometric shapes on a sea of double crochet. They have equal impact in a single- or double-row feature or edge, or as a full fabric.

SKILLS TAKE AWAY | Making shapes from grouping textured stitches

Pattern

Special stitch: Berry stitch (bry) – yarn over, insert hook, yarn over and pull up a loop; yarn over and pull through only one loop (you will now have 3 loops on the hook); yarn over, insert hook, yarn over and pull up a loop; yarn over and pull through all 5 loops remaining on the hook.

Ch 20.

Row 1: 1dc in 2nd ch from hook, 1dc in each ch to end, turn – 19dc.

Row 2: 1ch (does not count as first stitch), 1dc in each st to end, turn – 19dc.

Row 3: 1ch (does not count as first stitch), 3dc, 1 sl st, 1bry, 1 sl st, 7dc, 1 sl st, 1bry, 1 sl st, 3dc, turn.

Row 4: As Row 2.

Row 5: 1ch, 2dc, [1 sl st, 1bry] x2, 1sl st, 5dc, [1 sl st, 1bry] x 2, 1 sl st, 2dc, turn.

Row 6: As Row 2.

Row 7: 1ch, 1dc, [1 sl st, 1bry] x 3, 1 sl st, 3dc, [1 sl st, 1bry] x 3, 1 sl st, 1dc, turn.

Row 8: As Row 2.
Row 9: As Row 5.
Row 10: As Row 2.
Row 11: As Row 3.
Row 12: As Row 2.

Pattern repeats Rows 3–12 in sequence.

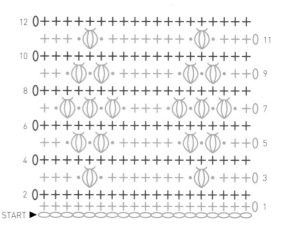

Abbreviations

A list of common abbreviations is given on page 94. Below are some special ones used in this stitch pattern.
bry = berry

Chart key

⬭ chain
• slip stitch
+ double crochet
▯ berry
▶ start

Note

• Each berry will have a slip stitch on either side.
• The berries themselves emerge on the other side of the fabric as you work, so you will have the wrong side facing you on the bobble row. The fabric is not reversible.
• Each row of berries is followed by a row of double crochet.

Diabobs

DIABOBS ARE BOBBLES THAT EMERGE OVER TWO ROWS TO MAKE DIAMOND SHAPES.

On the first row the bobbles grow from their base to their widest part, and on the second row, they close up again to complete the bobble shape. The 2-row bobbles themselves are relatively flat, so the character of the fabric is more lacy than textural.

SKILLS TAKE AWAY | Increasing and decreasing

Pattern

Ch 21.

Row 1: 1dc in 2nd ch from hook, 1dc in each ch to end, turn – 20sts.

Row 2: 1ch, 1dc in each st to end, turn – 20sts.

Row 3: 3ch (counts as first st), sk 1st, [3tr in next st, sk 2sts] x 5, 3tr in next st, sk 1st, 1tr in last st – 20sts inc turning chain.

Row 4: 4ch, [3trtog, 2ch] x 5, 3trtog, 1ch, 1tr in top of turning chain in row below.

Row 5: 1ch, 1dc in first tr, 1dc in next 1-ch sp, [2dc in next 2-ch sp] x 5, 1dc in next 1-ch sp, 1dc in top of turning chain in row below, turn – 20sts

Row 6: As Row 2.

Repeat Rows 3–6. (There are 18 rows in the crocheted swatch.)

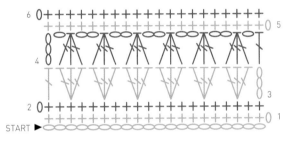

Abbreviations

A list of common abbreviations is given on page 94. Below are some special ones used in this stitch pattern.
3trtog = 3 trebles together (see page 21)

Chart key

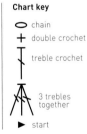

○ chain

+ double crochet

| treble crochet

⋀ 3 trebles together

▶ start

Polkabobs

THE KEY FEATURE OF THE POLKABOBS IS
THE COLOUR CHANGE. IN THE TWO-
COLOUR SWATCH THE SPOT YARN IS
HIDDEN INSIDE THE BACKGROUND YARN
AND EMERGES AS A BOBBLE WHEN
NEEDED.

The technique shown in the steps is
suitable for working with just two colours
in a row; the colour not in use at the
moment is encased within the stitches
being worked. This produces a reversible
fabric. When using more than two colours
in the row, as in the multicoloured swatch,
you use a method called intarsia (see page
54), which involves fastening a contrasting
yarn when needed and then fastening it off.

SKILLS TAKE | Changing colour
AWAY | mid-row

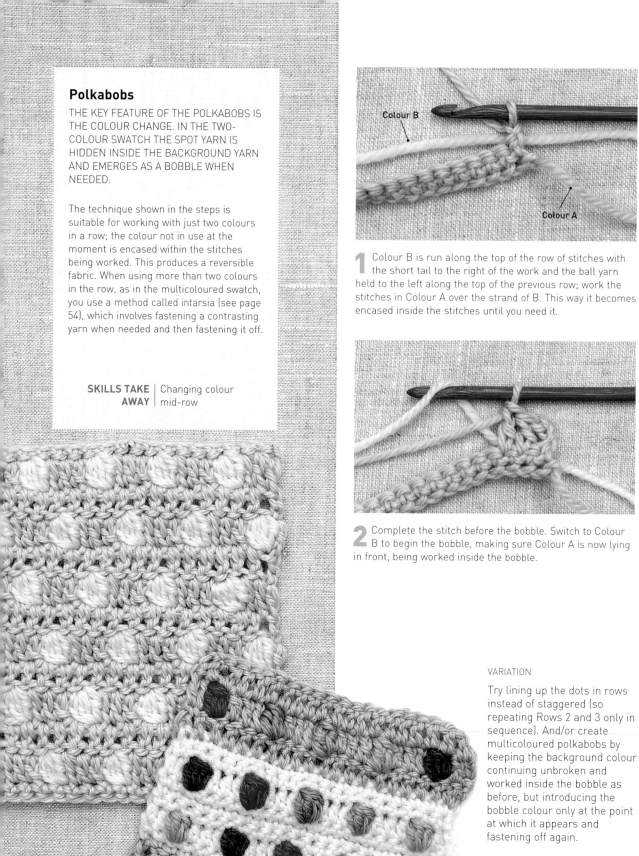

1 Colour B is run along the top of the row of stitches with
the short tail to the right of the work and the ball yarn
held to the left along the top of the previous row; work the
stitches in Colour A over the strand of B. This way it becomes
encased inside the stitches until you need it.

2 Complete the stitch before the bobble. Switch to Colour
B to begin the bobble, making sure Colour A is now lying
in front, being worked inside the bobble.

VARIATION

Try lining up the dots in rows
instead of staggered (so
repeating Rows 2 and 3 only in
sequence). And/or create
multicoloured polkabobs by
keeping the background colour
continuing unbroken and
worked inside the bobble as
before, but introducing the
bobble colour only at the point
at which it appears and
fastening off again.

The resting yarn lies along the top of the work, to be 'swallowed' inside the working stitch

3 Work your 4-post bobble, and switch back to Colour A (emerging from the left-hand side of the bobble) for the final yarn-over to pull through all 5 loops, bringing Colour B in front again to carry on being worked inside the stitches.

Tip

The working colour comes up from behind, and the 'sleeping' colour lies in front – swap them over each time you change.

Pattern

Special stitch: 4-post bobble (as 3-post bobble described on page 33 but with a 4th unfinished treble before completion), written here as 'bbl'.

In Col A, Ch 20.

Row 1: 1dc in 2nd ch from hook, 1 dc in each ch to end, turn – 19sts. Do not fasten off.

Row 2: 3ch, (turning chain counts as first stitch), Introducing Col B inside stitching, work 1tr in each of next 2 st, [switch working yarn to Col B, in next st work 1bbl with final yo in Col A, running Col B along inside each st, 1tr in each of next 3 st] x 4, turn – 4 bbl and 15 tr (including the turning chain at the beginning of the row).

Row 3: 3ch, running Col B along inside each stitch, 1tr in each st to end (taking care to work one into the turning chain of the row below), turn – 19sts including turning chain at the beginning of the row.

Row 4: In col A and continuing to run col B along inside the st, 3ch, [switch working yarn to Col B, in next st work 1bbl with final yo in Col A, running Col B along inside each st, 1tr in each of next 3 st] x 5 omitting last 2 tr, turn – 5 bbl and 14tr including the turning ch.

Repeat Row 3, 2, 3, 4 in that order for as long as you like. The illustrated sample has 13 rows.

Abbreviations

A list of common abbreviations is given on page 94. Below are some special ones used in this stitch pattern.
bbl = 4-post bobble (see 'Special stitch')

Chart key

⬭ chain

✛ double crochet

🇹 treble crochet

⬮ 4-post bobble

▶ start of row

Two-colour

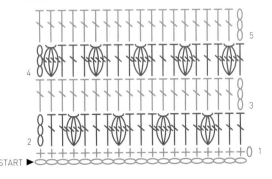

START ▶

Long and Leaning

THIS BOBBLE STRETCHES OUT LONG, AND LEANS RIGHT OVER.

Using an extra-tall stitch (the double treble), the bobble has a slimline silhouette with a leaf- or petal-like appearance. When combined with plenty of chain spacing, it creates an openwork design that may be seen as flowers or palm trees. Worked in 2-bobble clusters, with extra-large spaces in between that allow the bobbles to fan out, the pattern repeat emerges in its full glory only after four or five rows – so stick with it!

SKILLS TAKE AWAY | Using chains in openwork

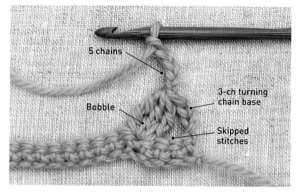

1 First make your foundation chain and a row of double crochet as Row 1. To begin Row 2, work the turning chain, and skipping the base of the chain and two more stitches, make a long, leaning bobble into the next stitch. Then work 5 chains.

2 To complete the 'paired' bobbles, work your next bobble into the same place as the last. The 5 chains you made before it will force the tops of the two bobbles apart, resulting in them leaning away from one another. Make no further chains before starting the next bobble pair.

VARIATION

For a different effect, use two colours (see above left). Work three rows of double crochet in Colour A first, changing to Colour B for the three rows that create the leaf effect (Rows 2, 3 and 4 in the instructions), before returning to Colour A for three more rows of double crochet. This creates a deep, flat stripe that emphasizes the petal shapes.

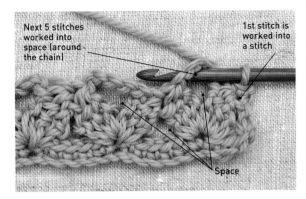

Next 5 stitches worked into space (around the chain)

1st stitch is worked into a stitch

Space

3 In Row 3, the first double crochet stitch is worked into the top of the treble stitch below, and the rest of the stitches are made into the spaces rather than into any stitches.

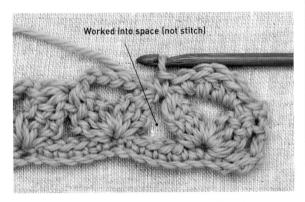

Worked into space (not stitch)

4 Even the double crochet between the bobbles is worked into a space. TIP: Keep counting your stitches, and take care not to lose the edge stitches as you work the rows.

Pattern

Special stitch: Long and Leaning Bobble stitch – 3dtrtog in same stitch, written here as 'llbbl'. *Yo twice, insert hook, yo and pull through, (yo and pull through 2 loops) twice, repeat from * twice (all posts worked into same base), yo and pull through all 4 loops.

Ch 20.

Row 1: 1dc in 2nd chain from hook, 1dc in each ch to end, turn – 19sts.

Row 2: 3ch (turning chain counts as first stitch) sk 2sts, *(1 llbbl, 5ch, 1 llbbl) in next st, sk 5sts, repeat once from *, (1 llbbl, 5ch, 1 llbbl) in next st, sk 2sts, 1tr in last st, turn.

Row 3: 1ch (turning chain does NOT count as first stitch), 1dc in top of tr, *(1dc, 1htr, 1tr, 1htr, 1dc) in next 5-ch sp, 1dc in next sp between 2 llbbl, repeat once from *, (1dc, 1htr, 1tr, 1htr, 1dc) in next 5-ch sp, 1dc into top of turning chain, turn.

Row 4: 5ch (turning chain counts as first stitch and 2 skipped stitches), 1 llbbl into base of turning chain, *sk 5sts, 1 llbbl into next st (Note: this l llbbl is worked into the centre of 3 dc sts), 5ch, 1 llbbl into same st as last llbbl, repeat once from *, sk 5sts, 1 llbbl into next st, 2ch, 1tr into top of last st, turn.

Row 5: 3ch (counts as first stitch), (1htr, 1dc) into 2-ch sp, *1dc in next sp between two llbbl, (1dc, 1htr, 1tr, 1htr, 1dc) in next 5-ch sp, repeat once from *, 1dc in next sp between two llbbl, (1dc, 1htr) in next 2-ch sp, 1tr in top of turning chain, turn.

Repeat Rows 2–5.

Abbreviations

A list of common abbreviations is given on page 94. Below are some special ones used in this stitch pattern.
llbbl = long and leaning bobble (see 'Special stitch')

Chart key

○ chain
+ double crochet
╤ half treble crochet
╪ treble crochet
⬥ long and leaning bobble
▶ start

One-colour swatch

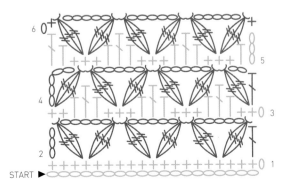

START ▶

Windmills

THESE WINDMILLS RECALL THE DECREASING AND INCREASING TECHNIQUES PRACTISED IN THE DIABOB PATTERN (SEE PAGE 41). BUT IN ADDITION, THEY INTRODUCE A NIFTY LITTLE 'TRAVELLING' HORIZONTAL BOBBLE IN BETWEEN THAT IS FUN TO DO AND WILL EXTEND YOUR OPENWORK SKILLS.

Originally appearing in old-fashioned lacy linen wear, this stitch nevertheless translates well into the chunkier yarns more in favour today. Although different, you'll find it is really just another variation on the theme of multiple posts being drawn together top and bottom. This little sideways bobble will be a useful addition to your growing repertoire of stitches.

SKILLS TAKE AWAY | Using bobbles in openwork

1 After completing Rows 1 and 2 in Colour A, change to Colour B in the last yarn-over. Make 4 chains (representing the first stitch, plus a 1-ch space), then work the next three trebles together, effectively decreasing by two stitches (see page 21).

3rd chain from hook

2 To make up for the stitches lost in the decrease and even things out, create the travelling bobble. Do this by first working 3 chains on top of the little triangle created by the decrease, yarning over and inserting the hook in 3rd chain from the hook.

VARIATION

As a variation on this stitch you could take out the plain bands and just keep the windmills (see bottom left). Make 20 chains to begin and then, starting at Row 3, repeat Rows 3 and 4 in sequence.

3 Yarn over again and pull up a loop, giving you three loops on the hook. Yarn over and pull through two loops, leaving you with two loops on the hook. Yarn over and reinsert in same place as before, then repeat.

4 Finally, yarn over and pull through all three loops on the hook and work your next decrease as before. The bobble becomes horizontal and straddles the space created by the decrease.

Tips

When making the increases on the next row, work them into the tighter stitch closest to the bobble to the right of the triangle.

Pattern

Special stitch: tbob (travelling bobble) – 3ch, yo, insert hook in 3rd ch from hook, yo and pull up a loop, yo and pull through 2 loops, yo and insert hook in same place as before, yo and pull through 2 loops, yo and pull through all 3 loops on the hook.

In Col A, ch 21.

Row 1: 1dc in 2nd ch from hook, 1dc in each ch to end, turn – 20sts.

Row 2: 1ch (turning chain does not count as first stitch), 1dc in each st to end, changing to Colour B in last yo, turn – 20sts.

Row 3: In Colour B, 4ch (turning chain counts as first stitch plus one chain), [3trtog, 1tbob] x 5, 3trtog, 1ch, 1tr, turn.

Row 4: 3ch (turning chain counts as first stitch), sk 1 ch, 3tr in top of first decrease of row below, [sk tbob, 3tr in top of next decrease in row below] x 5, sk 1ch, 1tr in top of turning chain from row below, changing to Colour A in last yo, turn.

Row 5: In Colour A, 1ch (turning chain does not count as first stitch), 1dc in each st to end, turn – 20sts.

Row 6: As Row 5, changing to Colour C in last yo.

Repeat Rows 3–6.

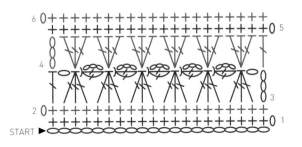

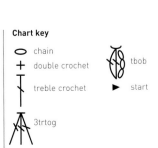

POPCORN WITH
RIBS
see page 52

POPCORN
TULIPS
see page 61

SCATTERED
CORN
see page 50

POP CIRCLES
see page 53

Popcorns

Popcorns stick out a mile. Like bobbles, they may have any number of posts (though usually five). But popcorns are multiple complete treble stitches drawn together with a single loop, making a much bigger bump. They are the cheeky, jolly extroverts of the craft, arguably having more impact when used sparingly, yet their big personalities may be channelled into a surprising range of effects from the 'trad' to the 'mad'. They have popped up on bedspreads and shawls, handbags and hats down the decades and continue to inspire designers creating items from household to haute couture.

5-post popcorn

POPCORNS ARE RAISED, ROTUND AND SHAPED LIKE A TEACUP. THE INITIAL STAGE IS EXACTLY LIKE MAKING AN INCREASE OR A FAN STITCH BECAUSE THE TREBLES SPREAD OUT FROM THE SAME BASE.

Video clip

Watch the video clip for working a 5-post popcorn (see page 49). This helpful visual reference will guide you through the process. To link to the video, use your mobile phone to scan the QR code on page 96.

Working a standard 5-post popcorn

1 In the space indicated by the pattern, make 5 trebles – yes, 5! You might wonder how you can fit 5 trebles in the one stitch, but you'll see that the stitch will expand to fit. The trebles create a fan (indeed, this is exactly how you do make a fan!).

2 The next move might feel a little counter-intuitive because you need to remove the hook from the work altogether. It's not for long though, as you'll see (unless your best friend suddenly calls right at that moment).

3 Go back to the very first treble you made in your fan and reinsert the hook under both loops of the stitch. Of course, try not to tug on that abandoned loop at the end or it will come undone.

4 .Now get the abandoned loop safely back on the hook. Yarn over and pull a loop up through the loops on the hook. You'll see it scrunches all the trebles together and makes a very three-dimensional clump that actually forms a little cup shape – the popcorn.

Scattered Corn

A SIMPLE INTRODUCTION TO USING POPCORNS, THIS 'SCATTERED' CONFIGURATION ECHOES THE POLKABOB PATTERN ON PAGE 42.

Alternating rows of textured and plain stitches makes the popcorns all appear on the same side of the fabric. The popcorn position on the row alternates, creating the staggered motif repeat.

SKILLS TAKE AWAY | Working multiple stitches into one base, positioning motifs in a staggered configuration

Pattern

Special stitch: 5-post popcorn (pc) – see page 49.

Ch 21 (multiple of 4 + 3).

Row 1: 1tr in 4th ch from hook, 17tr, turn – 19sts.

Row 2: 3ch (turning chain counts as first stitch), 2tr, [1pc, 3tr] x 4, turn – 15tr and 4pc.

Row 3: 3ch (turning chain counts as first stitch), 18tr, turn – 19sts.

Row 4: 3ch (turning chain counts as first stitch), [1pc, 3tr] x 4, 1pc, 1tr in top of turning chain, turn – 14tr and 5pc.

Repeat in the following sequence: Row 3, Row 2, Row 3, Row 4.

The swatch shown here has 11 rows.

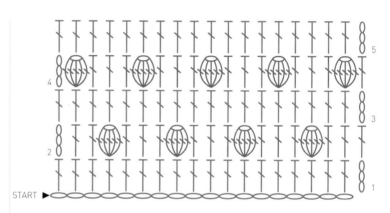

Abbreviations

A list of common abbreviations is given on page 94. Below are some special ones used in this stitch pattern.
pc = 5-post popcorn (see page 49)

Chart key

⚬ chain

⊤ treble crochet

⬭ 5-post popcorn

▶ start

Corn Rows

NOW THE CORN REALLY STARTS POPPING! THIS PATTERN INTRODUCES A 'V' STITCH BETWEEN EACH POPCORN.

An openwork technique that creates greater textural contrast, as well as letting in a little light and air. It also allows for more drape – much better for luxury wraps and cosy afghans.

SKILLS TAKE AWAY | The 'V' stitch used in openwork/lace patterns

Pattern

Special stitches:

5-post popcorn (pc) – see page 49.
'V'-stitch – 1 treble, 1 chain, 1 treble all worked into same stitch.

Ch 18 (multiple of 4 + 1).

Row 1: 1dc in 2nd ch from hook, 16dc, turn – 17sts.

Row 2: 4ch (counts as first stitch plus 1ch), *sk 1st, 1pc, sk 1st, 1 'V'-stitch in next st, repeat from * x 2, sk 1st, 1pc, 1ch, sk 1st, 1tr, turn – 2tr, 3 'V'-stitches and 4pc.

Row 3: 1ch, 17dc, turn – 17sts.

Repeat Rows 2 and 3 in sequence.

The swatch shown here has 13 rows.

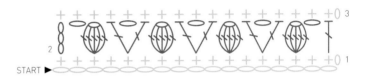

Abbreviations

A list of common abbreviations is given on page 94. Below are some special ones used in this stitch pattern.
pc = 5-post popcorn (see page 49)

Chart key

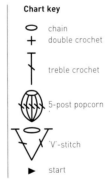

⬭	chain
+	double crochet
⊤	treble crochet
	5-post popcorn (see page 49)
	'V'-stitch
▶	start

Popcorn with Ribs

WHEN DESIGNING SOMETHING NEW, MIXING TECHNIQUES IS ALL PART OF THE FUN.

In this swatch, we double the bumps by using raised treble stitches in between, creating a ribbed effect that would make a great alternative sleeve cuff, collar, cowl or woolly hat fabric.

SKILLS TAKE AWAY | Working around the post to create raised stitches

Pattern

Special stitches:

Front-round-the-post treble (FPtr) – Yarn over, insert hook from right to left under the post of the st, yarn over and pull a loop through, then yarn-over and pull through 2 loops twice as with the standard treble stitch.

Back-round-the-post treble (BPtr) – Yarn over, insert the hook from behind the work, passing in front of the post on and out again behind the work, yarn over and pull a loop through, pull through 2 loops twice as with the standard treble stitch.

Ch 21 (multiple of 5 + 4).

Row 1: 1tr in 4th ch from hook, 1tr in each ch to end, turn – 19sts.

Row 2: 3ch (counts as first stitch), *2FPtr, 1tr, 1pc, 1tr, repeat twice, 2FPtr, 1tr in top of turning ch, turn – 8tr, 8FPtr and 3pc.

Row 3: 3ch (counts as first stitch), *2BPtr, 3tr, repeat twice, 2BPtr, 1tr in top of turning ch, turn – 19sts (11tr and 8BPtr).

Repeat Rows 2 and 3 in sequence.

The swatch shown here has 13 rows.

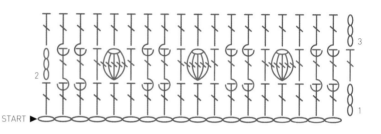

Abbreviations

A list of common abbreviations is given on page 94. Below are some special ones used in this stitch pattern.
BPtr = back-round-the-post treble (see 'Special stitches')
FPtr = front-round-the-post treble (see 'Special stitches')
pc = 5-post popcorn (see page 49)

Chart key

⊖ chain

┃ treble crochet

┣ front-round-the-post treble

┫ back-round-the-post treble

 5-post popcorn

▶ start

Pop Circles

THERE'S NOTHING MYSTERIOUS ABOUT THESE POP CIRCLES AND THEY MAKE SUPER-SPRINGY STOOL COVERS, FLOOR CUSHIONS OR COSY BEDROOM MATS.

The heavy texturing holds up well in a single shade for a cooler, classic look, but this could also be your chance to play fast and loose with your favourite palette.

SKILLS TAKE AWAY | Magic ring, controlled increasing to create a flat disc, working into a chain space, changing colour

Pattern

Special stitch: 5-post popcorn (pc) – see page 49.

In Col A make a magic ring (see page 18).

Rnd 1: 6dc into ring.

Rnd 2: 3ch (acts as first treble in first popcorn), complete the 4 remaining tr of the first pc, 3ch, (1pc, 3ch) into each remaining dc, sl st to close, fasten off – 6pc, 18ch.

Rnd 3: Join Col B in any 3-ch sp, 3ch (acts as first treble in first popcorn), complete the 4 remaining tr of the first pc, 3ch, 1pc in same 3-ch sp, 3ch, (1pc, 3ch, 1pc, 3ch in next 3-ch sp) x 5, join to top of first 3ch with a sl st, fasten off – 12pc, 36ch.

Rnd 4: Join Col C in 3-ch sp between first 2 popcorns in rnd below, 3ch, (acts as first treble in first popcorn), complete the 4 remaining tr of the first pc, 3ch, * in next 3-ch sp work (1pc, 3ch, 1pc, 3ch), in next ch-sp work 1pc, 3ch, repeat from * x 4, in next 3-ch sp work (1pc, 3ch, 1pc, 3ch) , join to top of first 3ch with a sl st, fasten off – 18pc, 54ch.

START

Abbreviations

A list of common abbreviations is given on page 94. Below are some special ones used in this stitch pattern.
pc = 5-post popcorn (see page 49)
3-ch sp = three-chain space

Chart key

⬯ chain
• slip stitch
✛ double crochet
⊤ treble crochet
⬯ 5-post popcorn
◎ magic ring
▶ start

Poptarsia

THE INTARSIA TECHNIQUE IS USED TO INTRODUCE A NEW COLOUR MID-ROW, SO THAT YOU CAN MAKE PICTURES OR ABSTRACT SHAPES IN THE FABRIC AS YOU WORK.

Either carry the secondary colour along inside the first, to emerge when required, or introduce it at the point it should appear and drop it again at the back when returning to the main colour. The technique selected depends on the nature of the design. In this swatch, you get to practise both methods. The grape-coloured yarn is not inserted until the first popcorn and the background yarn is carried along inside the grapes.

SKILLS TAKE AWAY | Intarsia technique to change colour mid-row

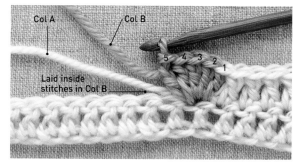

1 Introduce Col B at the first yarn-over of the first treble in the first popcorn. Bringing Col A in front, work it along inside the remaining four trebles of the popcorn so that it emerges ready to be used again to the left of the popcorn. Remove hook and insert into first of five stitches.

2 Swap Col A back in to yarn over and close the popcorn. This method encloses the popcorn completely, making the top chains of the row an unbroken line of Col A along the entire length.

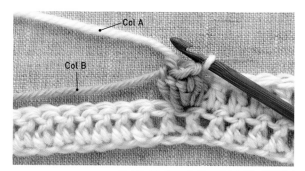

3 Leave Col B hanging at the back after the last popcorn on any row, picking it up again on the double crochet (reverse) row. Placing Col B along the top of the stitches, work double crochet in Col A as normal over the top of it.

VARIATION

This technique can be used to create any shape you like. Draft your own designs on squared paper. Note: 1 st or pc = 1 square wide and 2 squares high.

4 Wrap your double crochet stitches around Col B until it is repositioned for the next popcorn. When you have worked the required number of popcorns for that row, leave Col B hanging on the WS and continue to the end in Col A only. When it is no longer needed, fasten it off.

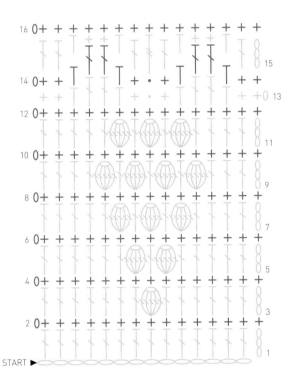

START ▶

Abbreviations

A list of common abbreviations is given on page 94. Below are some special ones used in this stitch pattern.

pc = 5-post popcorn (see page 49)

Chart key

⬯ chain
• slip stitch
+ double crochet
┬ half treble
⊥ treble crochet
⫯ double treble
🪢 5-post popcorn
▶ start

Tip

Take care to maintain the correct stitch count as you work your double crochet stitches on the 'reverse' rows, and when working the last stitch on any row into a turning chain.

Pattern

Special stitch: 5-post popcorn (pc) – see page 49.

Col A is the background colour, Col B is the popcorns/ grapes and Col C is the leaves at the top.

Note: Rows 4, 6, 8, 10, 12 and 16 are all as Row 2.

In Col A ch 17.

Row 1: 1tr in 4th ch from hook, 1tr in each ch to end, turn – 15sts.

Row 2: 1ch, 1dc in each st to end, turn – 15sts.

Row 3: 3ch (counts as first stitch), 1tr in each of next 6sts, in Col B 1pc in next st, change to Col A in last yo at top of popcorn, 1tr in each stitch to end, turn – 14tr and 1pc.

Row 5: 3ch (counts as first stitch), 1tr in each of next 5sts, *in Col B 1pc in next st, change to Col A in last yo at top of popcorn, 1tr next st, repeat from * once, 1tr in each st to end, turn – 13tr and 2pc.

Row 7: 3ch (counts as first stitch), 1tr in each of next 4sts, *in Col B 1pc in next st, change to Col A in last yo at top of popcorn, 1tr in next st, repeat from * twice, 1tr in each st to end, turn – 12tr and 3pc.

Row 9: 3ch (counts as first stitch), 1tr in each of next 3sts, *in Col B 1pc in next st, change to Col A in last yo at top of popcorn, 1tr in next st, repeat from * 3 times, 1tr in each stitch to end, turn – 11tr and 4pc.

Row 11: As Row 7.

Row 13: 1ch (does not count as first stitch), 1dc changing to Col C in last yo, *1dc, 1htr, 2tr, 1htr, 1dc,** 1sl st, repeat once from * to **, changing to Col A in last yo of last dc, 1dc in last st.

Row 14: As Row 13.

Row 15: 3ch (counts as first stitch), *1tr, 1htr, 2dc, 1htr, 1tr, **1dtr, repeat from * to **, 1tr in last st, turn – 15sts.

Popcorn Patterning

FREESTYLE YOUR POPCORNS TO EMULATE THE DEEP TEXTURAL CHARACTER OF A CABLE, SIMPLY BY POSITIONING THE POPCORNS JUST SO, ON A BED OF PLAIN TREBLES.

Make meandering lines, lozenges, polygons and borders. You could even fashion letter shapes to send a big corny message to someone you care about.

| SKILLS TAKE AWAY | Working with crochet charts to design and plan unique textured patterns |

Pattern

Special stitch: 5-post popcorn (pc) – see page 49.

Ch 16.

Row 1: 1dc in 2nd ch from hook, 1dc in each ch to end, turn – 15dc.

Row 2: 3ch (turning chain counts as first stitch), *1pc, 1tr, repeat from *(to end), turn – 7pc, 8tr.

Row 3: 1ch (turning chain does not count as first stitch), *1dc into tr, 1dc into top of pc, repeat from * x 6, 1dc into top of 3ch, turn – 15dc.

Row 4: 3ch (turning chain counts as first stitch), 1pc, 1tr in each of next 11sts, 1pc, 1tr in last st – turn (2pc, 13tr).

NB: All odd-number rows from Row 5 are as Row 3.

Row 6: 3ch (turning chain counts as first stitch), 1pc, 1tr in each of next 5sts, 1pc, 1tr in each of next 5sts, 1pc, 1tr in last st – turn (3pc, 12tr).

Row 8: 3ch (turning chain counts as first stitch), 1pc, 1tr in each of next 4sts, 1pc, 1tr 1pc, 1tr in each of next 4sts, 1pc, 1tr in last st – turn (3pc, 11tr).

Row 10: As Row 6.

Rows 12: As Row 4.

Row 14: As Row 2.

Swatch ends at Row 15. To continue in a repeat, begin again from Row 2.

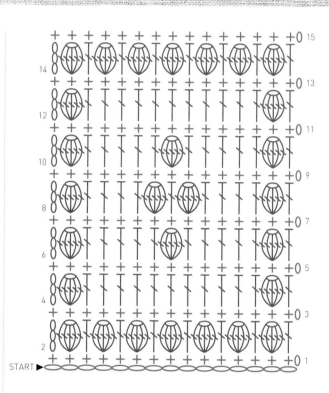

Abbreviations

A list of common abbreviations is given on page 94. Below are some special ones used in this stitch pattern.
pc = 5-post popcorn (see page 49)

Chart key

- ⬭ chain
- + double crochet
- ⊤ treble crochet
- 5-post popcorn (see page 49)
- ▶ start

Popcorn Peonies

YES, YOU CAN EVEN MAKE FLOWERS USING POPCORNS! THESE COMPACT, CUSHIONY ROSETTES WORK IN THE ROUND LIKE THE POP CIRCLES ON PAGE 53, BUT WITH A TWIST TO THE TECHNIQUE THAT TURNS POPCORNS INTO PETALS.

The peony bud works up fast in just two rounds, while the full bloom takes a little longer, with a third and final round that makes all the difference.

SKILLS TAKE AWAY | Working into the front and back loops separately – a technique common in flowers and Irish crochet

Peony bud

Full bloom

Pattern

Naming the loops: A crochet chain has a front, showing a row of 'V's and a back that appears to have a line of running stitches along its spine. Viewing the front horizontally, the back loops are at the top (furthest away) and the front loops at the bottom (nearest to you). The 'running stitches' on the back are called the back bumps.

Special stitch: 4-post popcorn (pc), closed in an alternative (slightly tighter) method as follows – work 4tr in same st, carefully remove hook from last tr and insert in top of first tr (under both loops of st), reinsert hook in dropped loop of 4th tr and firmly pull 4th tr through first tr.

PEONY BUD
In Col A, Ch 2.

Rnd 1: 6dc into 2nd ch from hook, sl st to close, fasten off.

Rnd 2: Join Col B in FLO of any st, *2ch, 1pc in FLO in same place as sl st, 2ch, sl st in FLO of next st, repeat from * to end working last sl st at base of first 2ch – 6 petals. Fasten off.

FULL BLOOM
Follow instructions as for small Peony Bud and continue to Rnd 3.

Rnd 3: 2ch, 1pc in BLO of =same st as last pc, 2ch, *sl st in BLO of next st, 2ch, 1pc in same place as sl st, 2ch, sl st in same place as before, 2ch, 1pc in same st as before, 2ch, repeat from * x 4, sl st in BLO of first st, 2ch, 1pc in same place as sl st, 2ch, sl st in same place, fasten off – 12 petals.

START

Abbreviations

A list of common abbreviations is given on page 94. Below are some special ones used in this stitch pattern.
BLO = back loop only
FLO = front loop only
pc = 4-post popcorn (see 'Special stitch')

Chart key

⌒ back loop
⌣ front loop
⬭ chain
• slip stitch
+ double crochet
⬮ 4-post popcorn
▶ start

Flopcorns

SECRETLY JUST AN OVERBLOWN (12-POST) POPCORN, THESE EXTRAORDINARY CREATURES ARE SURPRISINGLY VERSATILE.

Used sparingly, in cool and classic shades, the padded roundels will make a textural repeat that's subtle and interesting. Start to ramp up the numbers and density, however, and these draping circlets will begin to form a much more fulsome 'scaling' or tile. On top of that, because they flop down over the row below, you can use simple colour stripes to new effect too.

SKILLS TAKE AWAY | Working multiple stitches into the same base, changing colour for stripes

1 Work 12 trebles into the same space to form a fan shape.

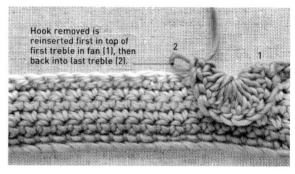

Hook removed is reinserted first in top of first treble in fan (1), then back into last treble (2).

2 Remove the hook and allow the whole fan to fall forward onto its face.

Yarning over and pulling through both loops closes the circle.

3 Insert hook into first treble, and then back into last treble, yarn over and pull through both.

VARIATION

Using the flopcorns more sparingly changes the character of the fabric (see blue swatch left). Here, the background base is (1dc, 1tr) repeated across the row, with (1tr, 1dc) in the following row. The flopcorns occur every 8th stitch on the row, and on every 6th row.

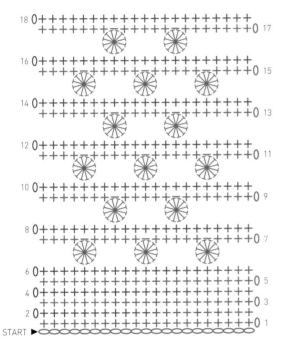

Push a finger underneath the flopcorn to push it outwards and form a convex roundel.

Note

When working flopcorns into a double crochet row, you may find that the first stitch after a flopcorn is very tight. Take care not to skip it by accident and keep a close tally of your stitch count on each row.

Pattern

Special stitch: Flopcorn (fc), a 12-post popcorn, as shown on these pages.

In Col A Ch 22.

Row 1: 1dc in 2nd ch from hook, 1dc in each ch to end, turn – 21sts.

Row 2: 1ch (does not count as first st), 21dc changing to Col B in last yo of last st, turn – 21sts.

Row 3: 1ch (does not count as first st), 21dc, turn – 21sts.

Row 4: 1ch (does not count as first st), 21dc changing to Col C in last yo of last st, turn – 21sts.

Row 5: As Row 3.

Row 6: 1ch (does not count as first st), 21dc changing to Col A in last yo of last st, turn – 21sts.

Row 7: 1ch (does not count as first st) 4dc, 1fc, 5dc, 1fc, 5dc, 1fc, 4dc, turn – 11dc, 3fc.

Row 8: As Row 2.

Row 9: 1ch (does not count as first st) 7dc, 1fc, 5dc, 1fc, 7dc, turn – 19dc, 2fc.

Row 10: As Row 4.
Row 11: As Row 7.
Row 12: As Row 6.
Row 13: As Row 9.
Rows 14: As Row 2.
Row 15: As Row 7.
Row 16: As Row 4.
Row 17: As Row 9.
Row 18: As Row 6.

Abbreviations

A list of common abbreviations is given on page 94. Below are some special ones used in this stitch pattern.
fc = flopcorn (see 'Special stitch')

Chart key

⬯ chain
+ double crochet
 flopcorn
▶ start

Picorns

THESE LITTLE BUMPS ARE VERY DINKY INDEED AS POPCORNS GO AND ARE STRUCTURALLY QUITE DIFFERENT, NOT REQUIRING ANY DOUBLE CROCHET OR TREBLE STITCHES AT ALL.

Relying wholly on chains and slip stitches, they're actually just a picot edge that doesn't stop at the border. Try out surface crochet here too.

SKILLS TAKE AWAY | Slip-stitching to join chains into loops, surface crochet to embellish

Pattern

Special stitch: Picorn – 1 double crochet, 3 chains, slip stitch into the first (bottom) chain, creating a loop.

Special note about working the row immediately above (and behind) the picorn: Work the first few dc on the row as indicated. For the dc corresponding with the picorn, work into the base of the picorn slightly to the right of it. The following dc will seem quite a leap away to the left (take care not to increase at this point by working a second stitch into the same picorn on the left). When yarning over for this stitch, be sure to bring the working yarn in front of the picorn.

Ch 18.

Row 1: 1dc in 2nd ch from hook, 1dc into each ch to end, turn – 17dc.

Row 2: 1ch (does not count as first stitch), 3dc, 1picorn, 3dc, 1picorn, 1 dc, 1picorn, 3dc, 1picorn, 3dc, turn – 13dc, 4picorns.

Row 3: 1ch (does not count as first stitch), 1dc in each st to end (see special note about working into back of picorn) – 17dc. NB: count your stitches here.

Row 4: 1ch (does not count as first stitch), 7dc, 1picorn, 1 dc, 1picorn, 7dc, turn – 15dc, 2picorns.

Rows 5 and 6: As Rows 3 and 4.

Row 7: As Row 3.
Pattern repeats from Rows 2–7.

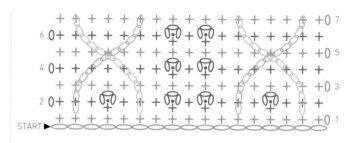

Abbreviations

A list of common abbreviations is given on page 94.

Chart key

chain

double crochet

picorn

start

Creating the Cable Effect

Surface crochet is a versatile technique for embellishing work after the main fabric has been established. Resembling an embroidery chain stitch, it can be used to spectacular effect with contrasting colours and it's also great in the same colour for fashioning faux cables, as here. Use it in a precise geometric way or to create more organic forms.

Simply insert your hook from front to back, yarn over at the back of the work and pull through a loop. Travelling along the fabric, insert again, yarn over, pull through to the front and then through the loop on the hook.

Popcorn Tulips

HERE YOU PRACTISE NOT ONLY YOUR 5-POST POPCORN FOR THE FLOWER BUD BUT ALSO A 2-POST LEANING BOBBLE FOR THE LEAVES, JUST TO KEEP YOU INTERESTED!

Despite appearances, there are no colour changes mid-row, just a straightforward stripe. A cute row of tulips works equally well as an accent or border.

SKILLS TAKE AWAY | Creating texture by alternating stitch heights on the row and front-round-the-post double crochet stitches.

Pattern

Special stitches:

5-post popcorn (pc) – see page 49.

2-post bobble (tbob) – *Yarn over, insert hook where indicated, yarn over and pull up a loop, yarn over and pull through two loops, (leaving two loops on the hook), repeat from * inserting hook in the same place as before, (three loops left on the hook), yarn over and pull through all three loops.

In Col A, ch 21.

Row 1: 1dc in 2nd ch from hook, 1dc in each ch to end, turn – 20sts.

Row 2: 1ch (does not count as first stitch), 1dc in each ch to end, changing to Col B in last yo of last st, turn – 20sts.

Row 3: 1ch (does not count as first stitch), 1dc in each ch to end, turn – 20sts.

Row 4: 1ch (does not count as first stitch), 1dc in each ch to end, changing to Col A in last yo of last st, turn – 20sts.

Row 5: As Row 3.

Row 6: 1ch (does not count as first stitch), 1dc in each ch to end, changing to Col C in last yo of last stitch, turn – 20sts.

Chart key

⬭ chain

+ double crochet

† treble crochet

⬭ 5-post popcorn

⬭ tbob

▶ start

Row 7: 3ch (counts as first stitch), sk 1, *(1tbob, 2ch, 1tbob) all in next st, sk 2, repeat from * x 4, (1tbob, 2ch, 1tbob) in next st, sk 1, 1tr in last st, fasten off. Do not turn.

Row 8: Join Col D in top of turning chain of row below – working same side of fabric again.

3ch (counts as first stitch), 1ch, *1pc in next 2-ch sp, 2ch, repeat from * x 4, 1pc in next 2-ch sp, 1ch, 1tr, fasten off. Do not turn.

Row 9: Join Col A in top of turning chain of row below – working same side of fabric again, 1ch (does not count as first stitch), 1dc in same stitch as join, 1dc in sp between turning chain and first pc, [1dc in top of pc, 2dc in next 2-ch sp] x 5, 1dc in top of last pc, 1dc in sp between last pc and tr at end of row, 1dc in top of tr, turn – 20dc.

Pattern repeats from Row 2–9.

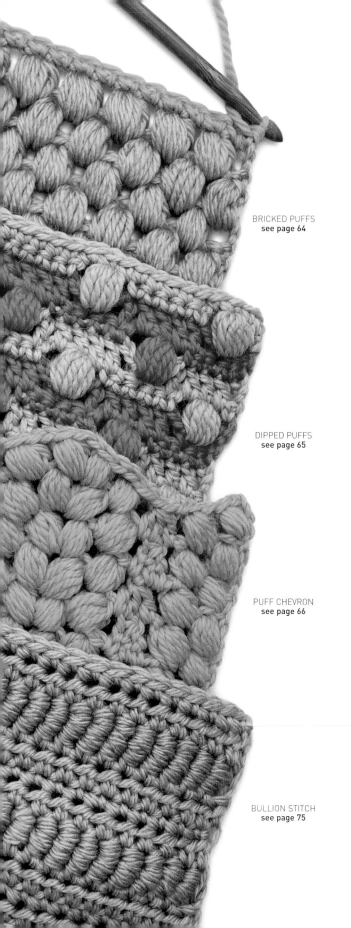

BRICKED PUFFS
see page 64

DIPPED PUFFS
see page 65

PUFF CHEVRON
see page 66

BULLION STITCH
see page 75

Puffs

Puffs are distinct from popcorns and bobbles in that they do not contain any part of a treble stitch. Indeed, they are rather a law unto themselves. The defining action in a puff is the drawing up of a longer loop, measuring the height by eye and intuition. This may seem daunting to the uninitiated, but you'll find that after a few deep breaths and two or three rows of practice, your puffs will quickly settle into uniformity as you find your own tension.

5-pass puff

THE LONG LENGTHS OF THREAD IN A PUFF RESEMBLE THE LUSTROUS EMBROIDERY SATIN STITCH AND CREATE A DEEP CUSHION OF FABRIC, USING UP COPIOUS QUANTITIES OF YARN.

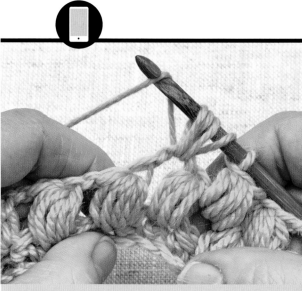

Video clip

Watch the video clip for working a 5-pass puff (see page 63). This helpful visual reference will guide you through the process. To link to the video, use your mobile phone to scan the QR code on page 96.

Working a standard 5-pass puff

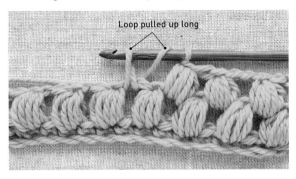

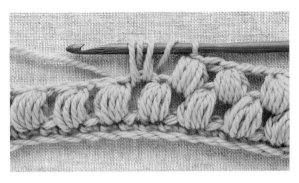

1 In the space indicated by the pattern, first yarn over, then insert your hook and yarn over once more as you do for a treble stitch. Pull the loop through as normal but then slide it up to the height of a treble stitch.

2 Repeat this action. You should now have 4 long loops on the hook.

3 Repeat the action three more times. You will have passed the hook through five times and have 11 loops on your hook. (For a 4-pass puff you will have 9 loops on the hook, and for a 6-pass you will have 13).

4 Finally, yarn over and pull through all 11 loops. You will note that this action alone does not really 'seal' the puff. Depending on the pattern, either you will make an additional chain to draw in the top, or the next stitch effectively does it.

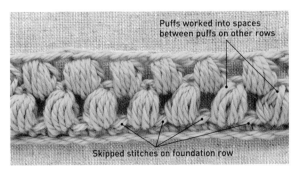

5 Read your pattern carefully because some patterns assume you make a chain at this point to finish off the puffing process. Be aware, however, that this chain is effectively another stitch and could play havoc with your stitch count in more complex designs.

6 The first row of a purely puffs fabric is a foundation, whether you are working directly into the chain or any other stitch. Either way, you will need to skip a stitch between each puff. In subsequent rows, you simply work into the chain spaces between the puffs (see Bricked Puffs, page 64).

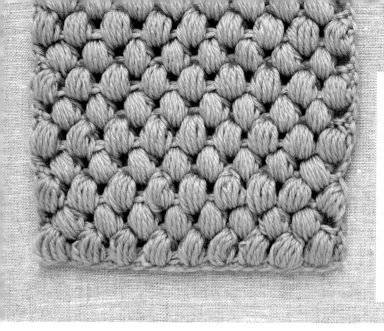

Bricked Puffs

THIS SIMPLE LAYOUT, WHERE PUFF POSITIONS
ALTERNATE IN A TWO-ROW REPEAT, REMAINS
A PERENNIAL FAVOURITE.

The resulting fabric has a luxurious texture, while
the long thread lengths bring out the lustre in
fibres with a sheen. Effective in a single shade, it
also lends itself to stripes and variegated colour.

SKILLS TAKE AWAY | Judging loop heights evenly

Pattern

Special stitch: 5-pass puff, see
page 63, written here as 'FPP'.

In Col A, Ch 20 (multiple of 2
plus 2, plus 1 turning chain).

Row 1: 1dc in 2nd ch from hook,
1 dc in each chain to the end
changing to Col B in last yo of
last st, turn – 19sts.

Row 2: 3ch (counts as first
stitch), [1FPP, sk 1st, 1ch] x 8,
1FPP, 1tr, turn – 9FPP, 8 x 1-ch
sp, 2tr.

Row 3: 3ch (counts as first
stitch), [1ch, 1FPP in next 1-ch
sp] x 8, 1ch, 1tr in top of t-ch
of row below, turn – 8FPP,
9 x 1-ch sp, 2tr.

Row 4: 3ch (counts as first
stitch), [1FPP in next 1-ch sp,
1ch] x 8, 1FPP, 1tr, turn – 9FPP,
8 x 1-ch sp, 2tr.

Rows 5–10: Repeat Rows 3 and
4 in sequence, changing to Col
A in last yo of last st.

Row 11: 1ch (does not count as
first stitch) 1dc in top of tr, [1dc
in top of FPP, 1dc in 1ch sp] x 8,
1dc in top of FPP, 1dc in top of
t-ch, fasten off – 19dc.

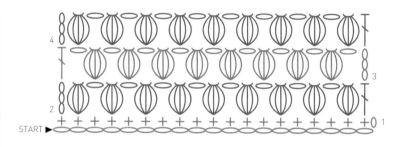

START ▶

Abbreviations

A list of common
abbreviations is given on
page 94. Below are some
special ones used in this
stitch pattern.
FPP = 5-pass puff (see
'Special stitch')
t-ch = turning chain
1-ch sp = one-chain space
(space made by working a
single chain)

Chart key

⬯ chain
+ double crochet

𝍑 treble crochet

⬭ 5-pass puff

▶ start

Dipped Puffs

THIS DESIGN IS A GREAT ALTERNATIVE TO THE PLAIN, TWO-COLOUR STRIPE.

Still changing colour every two rows, the dipped puff makes a 'glitch' in the colour stripe and keeps it interesting. It's formed by a simple change in stitch height that creates a notch for the puff to nestle in.

SKILLS TAKE AWAY | Using chains to create special effects

Pattern

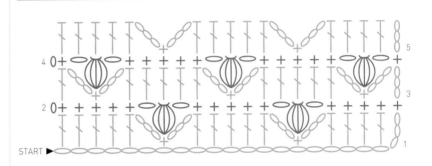

Special stitch: 5-pass puff, see page 63, written here as 'FPP'.

In Col A, ch 23 (multiple of 8, plus 5, plus 3).

Row 1: 1tr in 4th ch from hook, 3tr, [3ch, sk 1, 1dc, 3ch, sk 1, 5tr] x 2, changing to Col B in last yo of last st, turn.

Row 2: In Col B, 1ch (does not count as first stitch), [5dc, 1ch, 1FPP in dc in centre of dip, 1ch] x 2, 5dc, turn.

Row 3: 3ch (counts as first stitch – i.e. a tr), [3ch, sk 1, 1dc in dc, 3ch, sk 1, 1tr in dc, 1tr in 1-ch sp, 1tr in top of puff, 1tr in 1-ch sp, 1tr in dc] x 2, 3ch, sk 1, 1dc, 3ch, 1tr in last dc, changing to Col A in last yo, turn.

Row 4: In Col A, 1ch, (does not count as first stitch), 1dc in top of tr, 1ch, 1FPP in dc in centre of dip, 1ch, [1dc in each of next 5 tr, 1ch, 1FPP in dc in centre of dip, 1ch] x 2, turn.

Row 5: 3ch (counts as first stitch), [1tr in 1-ch sp, 1tr in top of puff, 1tr in 1-ch sp, 1tr in dc [3ch, sk 1, 1dc in the dc in centre of dip, 3ch, sk 1, 1tr in next dc] x 2, 1tr in 1-ch sp, 1tr in top of puff, 1tr in 1-ch sp, 1tr in

last dc, changing to Col B in last yo of last stitch in row, turn.

Rows 6–16: Repeat Rows 2–5 in sequence.

Row 17: 1ch (does not count as first stitch), 1dc in dc, [1dc in 1-ch sp, 1dc in top of FPP, 1dc in 1-ch sp, 5dc] x 2, 1dc in 1-ch sp, 1dc in top of FPP, 1dc in 1-ch sp, 1dc in dc, fasten off.

Abbreviations

A list of common abbreviations is given on page 94. Below are some special ones used in this stitch pattern.
FPP = 5-pass puff (see 'Special stitch')
t-ch = turning chain
1-ch sp = one-chain space (space made by working a single chain)

Chart key

◯ chain
+ double crochet
$\dagger$ treble crochet
🮲 5-pass puff
▶ start

Puff Chevron

EVERYONE LOVES A CHEVRON IN CROCHET AND KNITTING, AND THIS IS A VARIATION ON THE THEME USING PUFFS.

The structure of chevrons is peaks – formed by increasing – and troughs – formed by decreasing – separated by plain stitches. Here the puffs appear on the 'mountain tops' (a mountain top being a place where you need a bit of puff, right!).

SKILLS TAKE AWAY | Increasing and decreasing

Pattern

Special stitch: 5-pass puff, see page 63, written here as 'FPP'.

Ch 24 (multiple of 10 plus 4).

Row 1: 1FPP in 4th ch from hook, *1ch, sk 1, 1FPP, 1ch, sk 1, 3trtog, 1ch, sk 1, 1FPP, sk 1, 1ch**, (1FPP, 1ch, 1FPP) in next ch, repeat from * to **, (1FPP, 1tr) in last ch, turn.

Row 2: 3ch (counts as first stitch), 1FPP into base of t-ch, *1ch, 1FPP into next 1-ch sp, 1ch, 3trtog (first in 1-ch sp, 2nd in top of 3trtog in row below, and 3rd in foll 1-ch sp), 1ch, 1FPP in next 1-ch sp, 1ch**, (1FPP, 1ch, 1FPP) in next 1-ch sp, repeat from * to **, 1FPP in top of t-ch, 1tr in top of t-ch, turn.

Row 3: Repeat Row 2.

The swatch shown here has 11 rows.

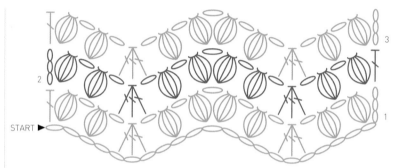

Abbreviations

A list of common abbreviations is given on page 94. Below are some special ones used in this stitch pattern.
3trtog = 3 trebles together (see page 21)
FPP = 5-pass puff (see 'Special stitch')
1-ch sp = one chain space (space made by working a single chain)
t-ch = turning chain

Chart key

⬭	chain
⊤	treble crochet
⋀	3trtog
◍	5-pass puff
▶	start

Note

This stitch benefits greatly from blocking (see page 27). Take care to pin out the peaks and troughs crisply and level with one another.

Puffs of Air

PUFFS ARE NOT CONFINED TO DENSE AND WOOLLY FABRICS, AS THIS MORE TRADITIONAL, LIGHT AND LACY STITCH ATTESTS.

With openwork designs such as this, the crochet chart really comes into its own and the colour-coded rows help you to keep track of where you are.

SKILLS TAKE AWAY | Practising doubles, trebles and double trebles on the same row; working with lace and openwork

Pattern

Special stitch: 4-pass puff, written here as 'fPP' – follow standard 5-pass puff instructions on page 63, but work one less pass, last yarn-over being pulled through 9 loops only.

Ch 18 (multiple of 8, plus 2).

Row 1: 1dc in 2nd ch from hook, *sk 3, (1tr, 1ch, 1tr, 1ch, 1 fPP, 1ch, 1tr, 1ch, 1tr) in next chain, sk 3, 1dc in next ch**, repeat from * to **, turn.

Row 2: 7ch (counts as 1tr, plus 3ch), *1dc into 2nd 1-ch sp (next to puff), 3ch, 1dc into next 1-ch sp (on other side of puff), 3ch, 1dtr into dc,** 3ch, repeat from * to **, turn.

Row 3: 4ch (counts as 1tr, plus 1ch), (1tr, 1ch, 1tr) into dtr, 1dc into 3-ch sp, (1tr, 1ch, 1tr, 1ch, 1 fPP, 1ch, 1tr, 1ch, 1tr) in next dtr, 1dc into next 3-ch sp, (1tr, 1ch, 1tr, 1ch, 1tr) into top of 4th ch, turn.

Row 4: 1ch (does not count as first stitch), 1dc into tr, 1dc into first 1-ch sp, *3ch, 1dtr in dc, 3ch, sk 1 1-ch sp, 1dc into next 1-ch sp** (next to puff), 3ch, 1dc into next 1-ch sp (on other side of puff), repeat from * to **, 1dc into top of t-ch, turn.

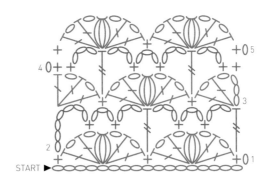

Abbreviations

A list of common abbreviations is given on page 94. Below are some special ones used in this stitch pattern.
fPP = 4-pass puff (see 'Special stitch')
1-ch sp = one-chain space (space made by working a single chain)
3-ch sp = three-chain space (space made by working three chains instead of a stitch)
t-ch = turning chain

Chart key

- ⬯ chain
- + double crochet
- ⊤ treble crochet
- ⊤ double treble crochet
- ⬭ 4-pass puff
- ▶ Start

Row 5: 1ch (does not count as first stitch), 1dc in first dc, sk 1 dc and 3ch, *(1tr, 1ch, 1tr, 1ch, 1 fPP, 1ch, 1tr, 1ch, 1tr)**, 1dc into 3-ch sp, repeat from * to **, 1dc into last dc.

Repeat Rows 2–5 in sequence.

Puff Cushion

THIS ADORABLE USE OF PUFFS GOBBLES UP YARN AND MAKES A THICK CUSHIONEY FABRIC THAT WOULD NEED NO FURTHER PADDING AS A SEAT COVER OR MAT.

Here, two DK yarns are used as one, with a 5mm hook, to create that two-colour look. It works up fast and uses no stitches other than the 2-pass puff. It would lend itself well to super-chunky yarns or even fabric strips for a rag rug.

SKILLS TAKE AWAY | Pulling a single loop through multiple loops on the hook, working two strands of yarn together as one

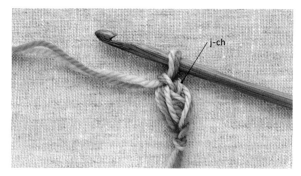

1 Using two strands together make a slip knot and one chain. *Slide loop on hook up long, (yarn over, insert hook in chain, yarn over and pull through, slide loop up to match first long loop) x 2. Yarn over and pull through five loops on hook, one chain to close.

2 Repeat the process of Step 1 from * as indicated in the patttern to establish the foundation row.

3 Row 1: create one 2-pass puff stopping short of the closing yarn-over; (yarn over, insert in third join-chain from hook, yarn over and pull up a long loop) x 3.

VARIATION

The same stitch in a single strand of super-chunky yarn gives a different character to the finished fabric (see bottom left).

4 Yarn over, pull through all loops on the hook.

5 Make one chain to close. One double puff completed. To make next double puff start again by sliding up the loop on the hook long and work as for Step 3 into next join-chain (do not skip any join-chains).

Tip

You might want to use a rug-maker's latch hook for this stitch, as it involves pulling a single loop through rather a lot of loops all together.

Pattern

Special stitches:

2-pass puff (tPP) – using two strands of yarn, make a slip knot and one chain. Pull up a long loop, *yo, insert hook through ch, yo and pull through, sliding loops up long, repeat from *, – should have 5 loops on the hook, yo and pull through all 5, 1ch to close.

Double puff (Dp) – work a tPP as before but do not yo and pull through the 5 loops, turning back on the foundation 'chain' of puffs, *yo and insert hook in 3rd j-ch from the hook, yo and pull up a long loop, repeat from * twice, – should have 11 loops on the hook, yo and pull through, 1ch to close – 1Dp worked.

Foundation Row: Work your next tPP into the ch at top of the last. Make 7 tPPs in a row, one on top of the other to create the foundation row.

Row 1: (1Dp in next j-ch) x 5.

Row 2: 1tPP, 6Dp, turn.

Repeat Row 2.

The swatch shown here has 7 rows.

Abbreviations

A list of common abbreviations is given on page 94. Below are some special ones used in this stitch pattern.
Dp = double puff (see 'Special stitches')
j-ch = join-chain – the top of one puff where it joins to the puff above
tPP = 2-pass puff (see 'Special stitches')

Chart key

⬯ chain

🪡 2-pass puff

🪡 double puff

► start

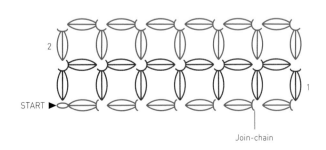

Join-chain

Puff Balls

WORKING 6-PASS, TREBLE-HEIGHT PUFFS, SECURED ON EITHER SIDE BY HALF TREBLE STITCHES, PERSUADES THE PUFFS TO TAKE ON A MORE SPHERICAL SILHOUETTE.

Arranging them on the row, with two plain stitches in between each, creates a 3-row repeat that produces an alluring diagonal texture.

SKILLS TAKE AWAY | Alternating stitch heights on the row to enhance 3D effect of puff

Pattern

Special stitch: 6-pass puff (sPP) – follow standard 5-pass puff instructions on page 63, but make an additional (6th) pass, making 13 loops on the hook.

Ch 16 (multiple of 3 plus 1).

Row 1: 1dc in 2nd ch from hook, 1dc in each chain to end, turn – 15 dc.

Row 2: 2ch (counts as first st), 1htr in next st, [1sPP, 2htr]x 4, 1sPP in last dc, turn – 5sPP, 10htr.

Row 3: 1ch (does not count as first st), [1dc in top of sPP, 1dc in each of next 2 htr] x5, 1dc in top of t-ch, turn – 15dc.

Row 4: 2ch (counts as first st), [1sPP, 2htr] x 4, 1sPP, 1htr in last st, turn – 5sPP, 10htr.

Row 5: 1ch (does not count as first st), 1dc in top of htr, [1dc in top of sPP, 1dc in each of next 2 htr] x 4, 1dc in top of t-ch, turn – 15dc.

Row 6: Slide up a long loop and complete the 6-pass puff by making 5 passes before drawing together (counts as first stitch), 2htr, [1sPP, 2htr] x 4, turn – 5sPP, 10htr.

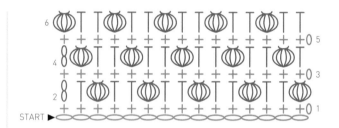

Abbreviations

A list of common abbreviations is given on page 94. Below are some special ones used in this stitch pattern.
sPP = 6-pass puff (see 'Special stitch')
t-ch = turning chain

Chart key

⬯   chain

+   double crochet

T   half treble crochet

🪔   6-pass puff

▶   start

Tips

Edge puffs – when a puff is the first stitch on a row, no need to make a turning chain, simply slide up a long loop and complete a 6-pass puff by making 5 passes before drawing together.
Border – when working a border around a puff ball fabric piece, stitches are worked around two strands of the edge puffs.

Puffs on the Side

THESE HORIZONTAL PUFFS FRAMED BY EXTENDED DOUBLE CROCHET STITCHES LOOK LIKE THE WINDOWS IN AN UPTOWN OFFICE BLOCK.

An easy and enjoyable stitch to relax into, with a refreshing 'take' on the puff. This dense fabric would work well for bags and baskets, cushion covers and seat pads.

SKILLS TAKE AWAY | Extended stitches

Pattern

Special stitches:

3-pass puff round the post (ThPP) – this is a puff worked around the post or stem of the treble stitch just made (instead of into the top of a stitch or into a one-chain space). [Yarn over, insert hook from right to left around the stem of the last treble worked, yarn over and pull up a long loop] x 3. Do not make an extra chain to fully close the puff.

Extended double crochet (Xdc) – this is a double crochet stitch but with a chain in the middle. Insert hook, yarn over and pull through as normal, leaving two loops on the hook, yarn over again and pull through one loop (1ch), yarn over once more and pull through last remaining two loops.

Ch 23 (multiple of 3 plus 2).

Row 1: 1dc in 3rd ch from hook, 1dc, [1Xdc, 2dc] x 6, 1Xdc in last ch, turn – 22sts.

Row 2: 2ch (counts as first Xdc), [1tr in next dc, 1ThPP round tr just worked, sk 1, 1Xdc] x 7, turn.

Row 3: 2ch (counts as first Xdc), [1dc into ThPP, 1dc into tr, 1Xdc into Xdc] x 7, turn.

Repeat Rows 2 and 3 in sequence.

The swatch shown here has 13 rows.

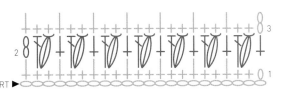

START ▶

Abbreviations

A list of common abbreviations is given on page 94. Below are some special ones used in this stitch pattern.
ThPP = 3-pass puff round the post (see 'Special stitches')
Xdc = extended double crochet (see 'Special stitches')

Chart key

⊖ chain
+ double crochet
┼ extended double crochet
𝖳 treble crochet
〭 3-pass puff round the post
▶ start

Spiked Puffs

THIS HIGHLY TEXTURED AND DENSE FABRIC IS A REAL YARN STASH BUSTER. COMBINING TWO TECHNIQUES – PUFFS AND SPIKES – THIS PATTERN REQUIRES A BIT OF CONCENTRATION AS YOU ESTABLISH ITS STRUCTURE. BUT IT'S WORTH THE EFFORT FOR ITS PERSONALITY!

The 3-pronged puffs spiking down over a flat bed of double crochet give it a sculptural quality that sets it apart – in a good way.

SKILLS TAKE AWAY	Spiked stitches, clustering puffs, creating one-chain spaces

1 Working a half treble into a space two rows below. Yarn over and insert hook into the space indicated, yarn over and pull up a loop, yarn over and pull through all 3 loops on the hook – intended to accentuate the space.

2 Working a spiked puff, or spuff – [yo and insert hook into the same 1-ch space as the half treble below, yo behind the work and pull up a long loop] x 4. You will now have 9 loops on the hook. Do not yo and close up.

Tip

With a pattern like this, where the row instructions are quite similar, cover up the next few lines with a bit of paper (and a paperweight), leaving visible only the row on which you're working. Use a hook with plenty of shaft length to accommodate 25 loops (i.e. not soft grip).

VARIATION

For a less elaborate use of spiked puffs, work them as evenly spaced singles (see 'Spuff' in 'Special stitches' on page 73).

4 long loops in next space 4 rows below

3 Make another spuff in the same 1-ch space as the next half treble, this time 4 rows below. You will now have 17 loops on the hook.

yo and pull through all loops

4 Work a 3rd spuff in the next htr/1-ch space 2 rows below, giving you 25 loops on the hook. Yarn over and pull through all loops and make one tight chain to draw the spuffs together at the top.

Pattern

Special stitches:

Spiked puff (Spuff) – work a 4-pass puff into the space indicated (either 4 rows or 6 rows below), you will have 9 loops on the hook but do not yo and draw loops together. Triple spiked puff (TSp) – 1 spuff in 1-ch sp 4 rows below dc just worked (9 loops on the hook), 1 spuff in next 1-ch sp, 6 rows below (17 loops on the hook), 1 spuff in next 1-ch sp, 4 rows below (25 loops on the hook), yo and pull through all 25 loops, work 1ch to fully close cluster and pull tight.

In Col A ch 20.

Row 1: 1dc in 2nd ch from hook, 1dc in each ch to end, turn – 19dc.

Row 2: 1ch (does not count as first stitch), [3dc, sk 1, 1ch] x 4, 3dc, turn – 15dc, 3 x 1-ch sp.

Row 3: As Row 2.

Row 4: 1ch (does not count as first stitch), 2dc, (sk 1 ch1, 1 htr into 1-ch sp 2 rows below, sk 1,1ch, 1dc,) x 4, 1dc, turn – 19sts.

Row 5: 1ch (does not count as first stitch), 2dc, (sk 1 ch1, 1dc into htr, sk 1,1ch, 1dc) x 4, 1dc, turn – 19sts.

Row 6: 1ch (does not count as first stitch), 2dc, [1htr into 1-ch sp 2 rows below, 1dc] x 8, 1dc changing to Col B in last yo, turn – 19sts.

Row 7: 1ch (does not count as first stitch), [3dc, 1 TSp] x 4, 3dc, turn – 19sts.

Staying in Col B, work rows 8–12 as rows 2–7, changing to Col B in last yo of last st.

Abbreviations

A list of common abbreviations is given on page 94. Below are some special ones used in this stitch pattern.
Spuff = spiked puff (see 'Special stitches')
TSp = triple spiked puff (see 'Special stitches')

Chart key

○ chain
+ double crochet
⊤ half treble

triple spiked puff

▶ start

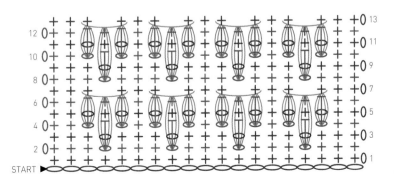

Solomon's Puffs

THE SOLOMON'S KNOT IS AN OLD CROCHET FAVOURITE AND BEARS A STRUCTURAL RELATIONSHIP WITH THE PUFF CUSHION ON PAGE 68.

Both require you to elongate loops and learn to regulate your tension by relaxing and working rhythmically. Here, the classic Solomon structure is worked in slimline puffs instead of knots.

SKILLS TAKE AWAY | The structure of the Solomon's Knot stitch

Pattern

Special stitch: Solomon's Puff (SP) – make one chain. Slide the loop on the hook up long (the height of a treble stitch), *yo, insert hook through ch at the base of the loop, yo and pull through, sliding loops up long, repeat once from * – should have 5 loops on the hook – yo and pull through all 5, 1ch to close. Solomon's Puffs are worked one in top of the other.

Foundation row: Make 6SP in a row, one on top of the other (the last SP forms the first 'upright' of Row 1).

Row 1: 1SP, folding back on foundation row, 1dc under both loops of 3rd j-ch, [1ch, 2SP, sk 1 j-ch, 1dc in next j-ch] x 2, 1ch, 1SP (forms last 'upright' of Row 1), turn – 7SP, 3dc.

Row 2: 2SP, working back along the row, 1dc under both loops of 4th j-ch, 1ch, 2SP, sk 1 j-ch, 1dc under both loops of next j-ch, 1ch, 2SP, sk 1 j-ch, dc in top of vertical SP at the end of the row, 1ch, 1SP (forms last 'upright' of Row 2), turn.

Rows 3–4: Repeat Row 2.

To finish, or cast off: 1SP, dc in 3rd j-ch, 1ch, 2SP, 1 dc in next j-ch, 2SP, 1dc in top of upright at the end of the row.

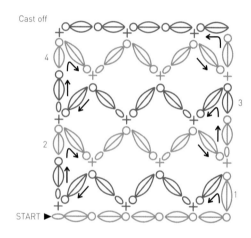

Cast off

4

2

3

1

START ▶

Abbreviations

A list of common abbreviations is given on page 94. Below are some special ones used in this stitch pattern.
SP = Solomon's Puff (see 'Special stitch')
j-ch = join-chain – the top of one puff where it joins to the puff above

Chart key

⬭ chain

+ double crochet

◯ Solomon's Puff

→ direction of crochet

▶ start

Note

The Solomon's puff is identical to the 2-pass puff in the Puff Cushion pattern on pages 68–69. Only here you will be using a single strand of yarn instead of two and this arrangement is a zigzag rather than a grid – you'll need to concentrate.

Bullion Stitch

BASED ON A TECHNIQUE FROM EMBROIDERY, THESE WRAPPED POSTS ENHANCE A YARN WITH A BIT OF A SHEEN OR LUSTRE.

Rather in a category of its own, it includes drawing a loop through multiple loops on the hook, like a traditional puff. You can use the bullion 'polka-dot' style in a sea of plain stitches, line it up shoulder-to-shoulder for a border with 'edge', or work it into a floral arrangement.

| SKILLS TAKE AWAY | Managing stitches that require multiple yarn-overs before insertion. Drawing a loop through multiple loops |

Pattern

Special stitch: Bullion (Bn) – wind yarn round hook 7 times, insert hook, yo, pull up a loop, yo and pull through 8 loops.

Ch 16.

Row 1: 1htr in 3rd ch from hook, 1htr in each ch to end, turn – 15sts (t-ch counts as first st).

Row 2: 2ch (t-ch counts as first st), 13Bn, 1htr, turn – 15sts.

Row 3: 2ch (t-ch counts as first st), 14htr, turn – 15sts.

Row 4: 1ch (t-ch does not count as first st), 15dc, turn – 15sts.

Row 5: As Row 3.

Repeat Rows 2–5 in sequence, finishing with row of dc (as Row 4).

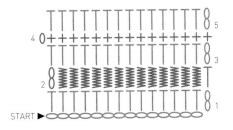

Abbreviations

A list of common abbreviations is given on page 94. Below are some special ones used in this stitch pattern.
Bn = bullion
t-ch = turning chain

Chart key

- ⌀ chain
- + double crochet
- T half treble
- ⧓ bullion
- ▶ start

Tips

Don't yarn-over too tightly. Go as loose as you dare, then you'll stand a chance of pushing all the loops over the hook.
Try pushing off four loops at a time, or even four, then three, then one. If all else fails, swap your crochet hook for a rug-maker's latch hook. Then it's really easy!

Chapter 3
The Projects

Now that you've become a master at creating crochet bobbles, popcorns and puffs you can turn you hand to the four inspirational projects in this section. Choose from a rug, bag, cushion or cowl – all designed with chunky textured bobbles, popcorns or puffs. Use the colour combinations suggested or choose a different mix to suit your own taste.

Puff Ball and Berry Rug

This super-squishy circular rug is both a treat for the feet and easy on the eye. A luxury of super-chunky puff balls and berries makes it a fun project that will keep you on your toes and maintain your interest.

You will need:

10mm crochet hook
Super-chunky yarn in 5 colours:
Colour A (Lemon): 240m (261yd)
Colour B (Cream): 200m (218yd)
Colour C (Pale Blue): 400m (435yd)
Colour D (Aqua Green): 500m (545yd)
Colour E (Grey): 80m (87yd)

Abbreviations

A list of common abbreviations is given on page 94. Below are some special ones used for this project.
bry = berry (see 'Special stitches')
rdc = reverse double crochet (see 'Special stitches')
pb = puff ball (see 'Special stitches')

Pattern
SPECIAL STITCHES:

Bobble berry (bry) – see page 40.

Puff ball (pb) – 6-pass puff (see page 70).

Reverse double crochet (rdc) – also known as **Crab Stitch** or **Binding Double Crochet** – continuing to work with RS facing you, 1ch (does not count as st) work an otherwise standard dc into previous stitch and continue to work 'backwards' all around.

In Col A, make a magic ring – see page 18.

(RS) Rnd 1: 3ch (counts as first st), 11tr in magic ring, sl st in top of 3ch to close – 12sts.

Rnd 2: 2ch (counts as first st), *(1htr, 1pb) in next st, 2htr in next st, repeat from * x 5, (1htr, 1pb) in next st, 1htr in last st, sl st to top of 2ch to close – 24sts.

Rnd 3: 1ch (does not count as first st) [1dc in next st, 2dc in foll st] x 12, sl st in first st to close, turn – 36sts.

(WS) Rnd 4: NB: berry rows are worked on the wrong side, so be sure to turn the work in the opposite direction on this round. [1 sl st in next st, 1bry in foll st] x 18 – 36sts (18bry, 18 sl st).

Rnd 5: 1ch (does not count as first st), 1dc in each st around, changing to Col B in last yo, sl st in first st to close – 36sts.

COL B
Rnd 6: 1ch (does not count as first st), [1dc in each of next 2 sts, 2dc in next st] x 12, sl st in first st to close – 48sts.

Rnd 7: [1 sl st in next st, 1 bry in foll st] x 24 – 48sts (24bry, 24 sl st).

Rnd 8: 1ch, 1dc in each st around, changing to Col C in last yo, sl st in first st to close, turn – 48sts.

COL C

(RS) Rnd 9: (NB this is a treble round which must be worked on the right side so be sure to have turned since previous round) 3ch (counts as first st), 1tr in each of next 2 sts, 2tr in next st, [1tr in each of next 3 sts, 2tr in foll st] around, sl st to top of 3ch to close – 60sts.

Rnd 10: 2ch (counts as first st), 1pb into base of 2 ch, *1htr in each of next 3 sts, (1htr, 1pb) in next st, repeat from * x 14, 1htr in each of next 3 sts, sl st in 2ch to close – 75sts.

NB Working dc will tighten up the edge slightly, helping to offset the puff rounds, which tend to make for enlarged stitches.

Rnd 11: 1ch (does not count as first st), [1dc in each of next 4 sts, 2dc in foll st] x 15, sl st in first st to close, turn – 90sts.

(WS) Rnd 12: [1 sl st in next st, 1bry in foll st] all around – 90sts (45bry, 45 sl st).

Rnd 13: 1ch (does not count as first st), 1dc in each st around changing to Col B in last yo, sl st in first st to close – 90sts.

COL B

Rnd 14: 1ch (does not count as first st), [1dc in each of next 5 sts, 2dc in foll st] around, with only 1dc in last st, sl st in first st to close – 104sts.

Rnd 15: [1 sl st in next st, 1bry in foll st] all around – 104 sts (52 bry, 52 sl sts).

Rnd 16: 1ch, 1dc in each st around, changing to col D in last yo, sl st in first st to close, turn – 104sts.

COL D

(RS) Rnd 17: 3ch (counts as first st), 1 tr in each of next 4 sts, 2 tr in foll st, [1 tr in each of next 5 sts, 2 tr in foll st] x 16, 1tr in each of last 2 sts, sl st in top of 3ch to close – 120sts.

Rnd 18: 2ch (counts as first st), 1htr in each of next 3 sts, [1pb, 1htr in each of next 4 sts] x 23, 1pb, sl st into top of 2ch – 120sts.

Rnd 19: 1ch, [1dc in each of next 7 sts, 2dc in next st] x 15, sl st in first st to close, turn – 135sts.

(WS) Rnd 20: [1 sl st in next st, 1bry in foll st] x 67, sl st in last st – 135sts (67bry, 68 sl st).

Rnd 21: 1ch, 1dc in each st around changing to Col E in last yo, sl st in first st to close, turn – 135sts.

COL E

(RS) Rnd 22: 1ch, [1dc in each of next 9 sts, 2dc in next st] x 13, 1dc in each of next 5 sts, sl st in first st to close, turn – 148sts.

(WS) Rnd 23: [1 sl st in next st, 1bry in foll st] x 74 – 148sts (74bry, 74 sl st).

Rnd 24: 1 ch, 1dc in each st around changing to Col D in last yo, sl st in first st to close, turn – 148sts.

COL D

(RS) Rnd 25: 3ch (counts as first st), 1 tr in each of next 9 sts, 2 tr in foll st, [1 tr in each of next 10 sts , 2 tr in foll st] x 12, 1tr in each of next 5 sts, sl st in top of 3ch to close – 161sts.

Rnd 26: 2ch (counts as first st) 1htr in each of next 3 sts, 1pb [1htr in each of next 4 sts, 1pb] x 31, sk last tr, sl st in top of 3ch to close – 160sts.

Rnd 27: 1ch, [1dc in each of next 11 sts, 2dc in next st], 1dc in each of next 3 sts, sk last st, sl st in top of first st to close, turn – 172sts.

(WS) Rnd 28: [1 sl st in next st, 1bry in foll st] x 86 – 172 sts (86bry, 86 sl st).

Rnd 29: 1ch, 1dc in each st around, changing to Col B in last yo, sl st in first st to close, turn – 172sts.

COL B

(RS) Rnd 30: 1ch, [1dc in each of next 12 sts, 2dc in foll st] x 13, 1dc in each of next 2 sts, sk last st, sl st in top of first st to close, turn – 184sts.

(WS) Rnd 31: [1 sl st in next st, 1bry in foll st] x 92, turn – 184 sts (92bry, 92 sl st).

(RS) Rnd 32: 1ch, [1dc in each of next 12sts, 2dc in foll st] x 14 , 1dc in each of next 2 sts changing to Col C in last yo, sl st in first st to close – 198sts .

COL C

(RS) Rnd 33: 3ch (counts as first st), 1 tr in each of next 12sts, 2tr in foll st, [1tr in each of next 13sts, 2tr in foll st] x 13, 1tr in each of next 2 sts, sl st to top of 3ch to close – 212sts.

Rnd 34: 2ch (counts as first st) [1 pb, 1htr in each of next 3 sts] x 52, 1pb, 1htr in each of next 2 sts, sl st to top of 2ch to close – 53 pbs, 159 htr.

Rnd 35: 1ch (does not count as first st), [1dc in each of next 14 sts, 2dc in foll st] x 14, 1dc in each of next 4 sts, sl st in first st to close, turn – 228sts

(WS) Rnd 36: 1ch (does not count as first st) (1bry in next st, 1 sl st in foll st) x 114, turn – 228 sts (114bry, 114 sl st).

(RS) Rnd 37: 1ch (does not count as first st), 1dc in each st around, changing to Col B in last yo, sl st in first st to close – 228sts.

COL B

Rnd 38: 1ch (does not count as first st), [1dc in each of next 15 sts, 2dc in foll st] x 14, 1dc in each of next 4 sts, sl st in first st to close, turn – 242sts.

(WS) Rnd 39: 1ch (does not count as first st) (1bry, 1 sl st) x 121, turn – 242 sts (121bry, 121 sl st).

(RS) Rnd 40: 1ch (does not count as first st), [1dc in each of next 16 sts,

Chart key

○	chain	┬	treble crochet
•	slip stitch		
+	double crochet		berry
┬	half treble crochet		puff ball
⊙	magic ring		

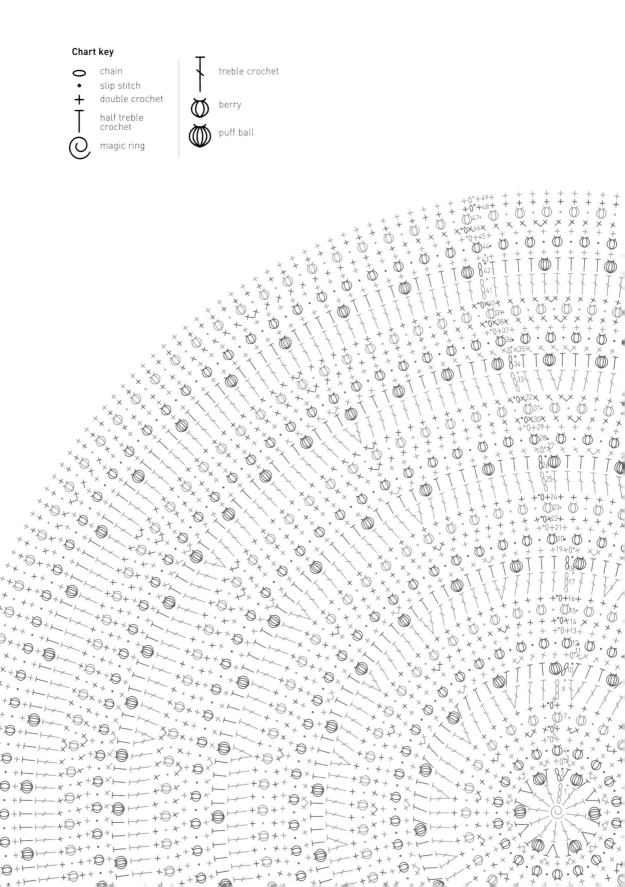

2dc in foll st] x 14, 1dc in each of next 4 sts, changing to Col A in last yo, sl st in first st to close – 256sts.

COL A

Rnd 41: 3ch (counts as first st), 1tr in each st around, sl st in top of 3ch to close – 256sts.

Rnd 42: 2ch (counts as first st), [1pb, 1htr in each of next 4 sts] x 63, 1pb, 1htr in each of next 3 sts, sl st in top of 2ch to close – 64pb, 192htr.

Rnd 43: 1ch (does not count as first st), 1dc in each st around, sl st in first st to close, turn – 256 sts.

(WS) Rnd 44: [1bry in next st, 1 sl st in foll st] x 128, turn – 256sts (128bry, 128 sl st).

(RS) Rnd 45: 1ch (does not count as first st), 1dc in each st changing to Col B in last yo, sl st in first st to close – 256sts.

COL B

Rnd 46: 1ch (does not count as first st), [1dc in each of next 17 sts, 2dc in foll st] x 14, 1dc in each of next 4 sts, sl st in first st to close, turn – 270sts.

(WS) Rnd 47: [1Bry in next st, 1 sl st in foll st] x 135, turn – 135bry, 135 sl sts.

(RS) Rnd 48: 1ch (does not count as first st), 1dc in each st around, changing to Col D in last yo, sl st in first st to close – 270sts.

COL D

Rnd 49: 1ch, 1rdc in each st around, sl st in first st to close, fasten off – 270rdc.

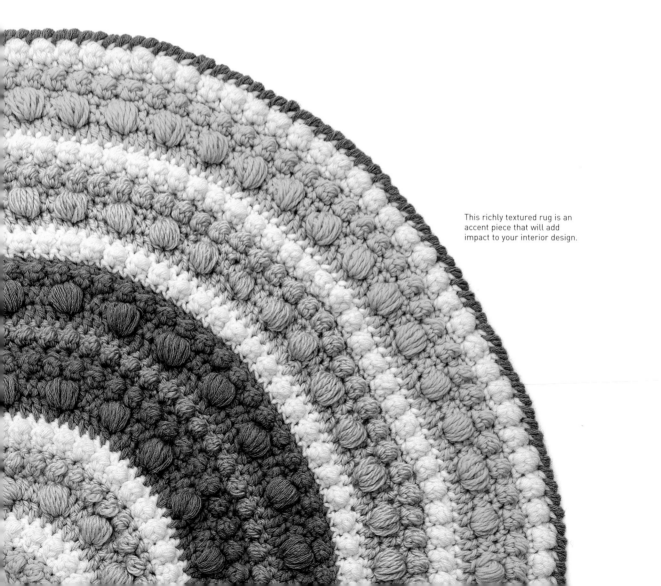

This richly textured rug is an accent piece that will add impact to your interior design.

Puff Bolster Cushion

Bolster cushions have long been a staple cushion style in fashionable homes around the world and their popularity shows no sign of waning. This quick-to-work-up, puff-stitch pattern can be made to any width simply by increasing or decreasing the number of puffs in a row, or any girth by increasing or decreasing the number of rows. Just be sure to match the row count on the main section with the perimeter stitch count on the circular end pieces (2 trebles to 1 row).

You will need:

10mm crochet hook
Super-chunky yarn in blue: 320m (348yd)
Bolster pad

Abbreviations

A list of common abbreviations is given on page 94.

Pattern

SPECIAL STITCHES:

Single puff – 2ch, slide up a long loop, *yo, insert hook into 2nd chain worked, yo and pull up a long loop, repeat from * twice, yo and pull through all 7 loops.

Double puff – 2ch, slide up a long loop, *yo, insert hook into 2nd chain worked, yo and pull up a long loop, repeat from * twice, yo, insert hook in next segment join , yo and pull up a long loop, (yo, insert hook in same segment join, yo and pull up a long loop) x 3, yo and pull through all 15 loops.

NB: The stitch pattern for the main section is on page 68 – 'Puff Cushion'.

MAIN SECTION

Foundation Row: 11 single puffs

Row 1: 1 single puff, 1 double puff into 3rd segment join from hook, 1 double puff into each remaining segment join, and into ch at base of first single puff in foundation, turn – 11 double puffs.

Rows 2–19: As Row 1.

Row 20: 3ch, (1tr into side of horizontal puff, 1tr into segment join) repeat to end), fasten off.

Turn work upside down (rotate 180 degrees), join yarn, work 3ch, and along bottom edge work 1tr into each puff and 1tr into each segment join.

Rotate work 90 degrees, make 1ch, and work 2dc around post of last tr worked and then 1dc into the side of each puff (picking up 4 strands of each), and 1dc into each segment join, and finally 2dc around post of tr at the other end – 42 sts, fasten off. Repeat on other long edge.

Chart key

○ chain
• slip stitch
+ double crochet
Ⅰ treble crochet
ⓒ magic ring
Ⓞ puff
▶ start

Main section

20 Top Border A

Border B
Double crochet down the long edge

19

START ▶

2

1

Border C - Treble crochet along bottom edge

END PIECES (MAKE 2)

Make a magic ring.

Rnd 1: 6 dc into ring, sl st to close.

Rnd 2: 1ch, 2dc into each st around, sl st to close – 12sts.

Rnd 3: 1ch, (1dc in next st, 2dc in foll st) x 6, sl st to close – 18sts

Rnd 4: 1ch, (1dc in each of next 2 sts, 2dc in foll st) x 6, sl st to close – 24sts.

Rnd 5: 1ch (1dc in each of next 3 sts, 2dc in foll st) x 6, sl st to close – 30sts.

Rnd 6: 3ch, 1tr in base of 3ch, (1tr in each of next 4 sts, 2tr in foll st) x 5, 1 tr in each of next 4sts, sl st to close – 36sts.

Rnd 7: 3ch, 1tr in base of 3ch, (1tr in each of next 5 sts, 2tr in foll st) x 5, 1tr in each of next 5 sts, sl st to close – 42sts.

JOINING

Working WS to WS, pin long edge of main piece around the perimeter edge of end piece, making sure short edges butt up against one another (no overlap and no gap). Join yarn and work 42dc through both pieces at the same time, matching stitch for stitch – 42 sts, sl st last st to first st to close the round. Repeat for second end piece.

FILLING

It is possible to purchase ready-made bolster pads. Buy this first and make your cover to fit. Or you can make your own by rolling up a sheet of foam like a Swiss roll. You will need to cover it in a tight sleeve of heavy calico or wadding in order to flatten out the bulky edge of the foam sheet and make it truly cylindrical.

End section

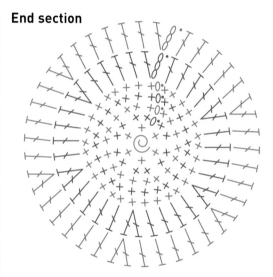

I-CORD STRAP TO LACE CLOSED

3ch, insert hook into 2nd ch from hook, yo and pull up a loop (2 loops on hook), insert hook into next ch, yo and pull up a loop (3 loops on hook), remove 2 loops from hook (you may wish to insert a cabling 'stay' or yarn marker to hold them, but it's quicker not to), yo and pull through the only remaining loop on the hook, replace one dropped loop, yo and pull through, replace the last dropped loop, yo and pull through.

Repeat from * until you have a length several centimetres longer than the length of the join, then fasten off. Join one end at the edge of the opening and then, inserting through the spaces in the fabric, snake the cord between the two open edges evenly until you reach the other side. Pull until the cord is almost straight, and tuck the free end in under the edge of the bolster. It should hold.

Puff Ball Bag

This round-bottomed, vintage-style handbag has lots of personality and makes use of the generous 6-pass puff pattern on page 70. Its irresistible character and puffiness are further enhanced by a padded lining in a colourful cotton and old-fashioned wooden handles.

You will need

6mm crochet hook
Chunky yarn in orange: 272m (296yd)

Abbreviations

A list of common abbreviations is given on page 94. Below are some special ones used for this project.
pb = puff ball (see 'Special stitches')
2pbtog = Two puff balls together (see 'Special stitches')

Tips

Use a stitch marker or a contrasting length of yarn to indicate the beginning of each round.

You will be working with the inside of the bag facing you for the entire puff ball section of the bag, as this pattern is worked in a circle from the base. Guard against inadvertently turning the other way after breaks.

Pattern

SPECIAL STITCHES

Puff ball (pb) – 6-pass puff (see page 70).

Two Puff balls together (2pbtog) – *In next double crochet, (yarn over, insert hook, yarn over and pull up a long loop) x 6**, skip next puff ball in the row below, repeat from * to ** once, yarn over and pull through all 26 loops on the hook.

Ch 12.

Rnd 1: 1dc in blo of 2nd ch from hook, 1dc in blo of each of next 9 ch, 3dc in blo of foll ch, rotate work 180 degrees (turn upside down) and work back along the underside of the same ch, 1dc in each of next 9 ch, 2dc in last ch, sl st to first dc in round to close – 24sts.

Rnd 2: 1pb in same place as sl st, 1dc in next dc, [1pb in next dc, 1dc in next pb] x 11, sl st in top of first pb in rnd to close – 24sts (12pb,12dc).

Rnd 3: 1ch (does not count as first stitch), 1dc in same place as sl st, [1pb into next dc, 1dc in next pb] x 5, (1pb, 1dc, 1pb) into next dc, 1dc into next pb, [1pb into next dc, 1dc into next pb] x 5, (1pb, 1dc, 1pb) into next dc, sl st to first dc in rnd to close – 28sts (14pb, 14dc).

Rnd 4: (1pb, 1dc, 1pb) in same place as sl st, 1dc in next pb, [1pb in next dc, 1dc in next pb] x 4, (1pb, 1dc, 1pb) in next dc, 1dc into next pb, 1pb in next dc, 1dc in next pb, (1pb, 1dc, 1pb) in next dc, 1dc into next pb, [1pb in next dc, 1dc in next pb] x 4, (1pb, 1dc, 1pb) in next dc, 1dc in next pb, 1pb in next dc, 1dc in next pb, sl st in first pb of rnd to close – 36sts (18pb, 18dc).

Rnd 5: 1ch (does not count as first stitch), 1dc in same place as sl st, *[1pb in next dc, 1dc in next pb] x 7, [(1pb, 1dc, 1pb) in next dc, 1dc in next pb] x 2, repeat from * omitting last dc, sl st to first dc in rnd to close – 44sts (22pb, 22dc).

Rnd 6: Place a marker, 1pb in same place as sl st, 1dc in next pb, [1pb in next dc, 1dc in next pb] x 8, (1pb, 1dc,

This delightfully bobbly bag is ideal for carrying your current crochet project and adds a dash of vintage flavour to your personal style.

1pb) in next dc, 1dc into next pb, [1pb in next dc, 1dc into next pb] x 10, (1pb, 1dc, 1pb) in next dc, 1dc in next pb, 1pb in next dc, 1dc in next pb, sl st in first pb of rnd to close – 48sts (24pb, 24dc).

Rnd 7: Place a marker,1ch (does not count as first stitch), 1dc in same place as sl st, [1pb in next dc, 1dc in next pb] x 8, *(1pb, 1dc, 1pb) in next dc, 1dc in next pb**, 1pb in next dc, 1dc in next dc, repeat from * to**, [1pb in next dc, 1dc in next pb] x 9, ***(1pb, 1dc, 1pb) in next dc, 1dc in next pb****, 1pb in next dc, 1dc in next dc, repeat from *** to ****, 1pb in last dc, sl st to first dc in rnd to close – 56sts (28pb, 28dc).

Rnd 8: (no increase) 1pb in same place as sl st, 1dc in next pb, [1pb in next dc, 1dc in next pb] x 27, sl st in first pb of rnd – 56sts (28pb, 28dc).

Rnd 9: (increase) 1ch (does not count as first stitch), 1dc in same place as sl st, [1pb in next dc, 1dc in next pb] x 10, (1pb, 1dc, 1pb) in next dc, 1dc in next pb, [1pb in next dc, 1dc in next pb] x 13, (1pb, 1dc, 1pb) in next dc, 1dc in next pb, [1pb in next dc, 1dc in next pb] x 2, 1pb in last dc, sl st in first dc of rnd to close – 60sts (30pb, 30dc).

Rnd 10: (no increase) 1pb in same place as sl st, 1dc in next pb, [1pb in next dc, 1dc in next pb] x 29, sl st in first pb of rnd – 60sts (30pb, 30dc).

Rnd 11: (no increase) 1ch (does not count as first stitch), 1dc in same place as sl st, [1pb in next dc, 1dc in next pb] x 29, 1pb in last dc, sl st in top of first pb in rnd to close – 60sts (30pb, 30dc).

Rnd 12: (no increase) 1pb in same place as sl st, 1dc in next pb, [1pb in next dc, 1dc in next pb] x 29, sl st in first pb of rnd – 60sts (30pb, 30dc).

Rnd 13: (decrease) 1ch (does not count as first stitch), 1dc in same place as sl st, [1pb in next dc, 1dc in next pb] x 10, 2pbtog in next 3 sts, 1dc in next pb, [1pb in next dc, 1dc in next pb] x 13, 2pbtog in next 3 sts, 1dc in next pb, [1pb in next dc, 1dc in next pb] x 2, 1pb in last dc, sl st in first dc of rnd to close – 56sts (26pb, 2 x 2pbtog, 28dc).

Rnd 14: (no decrease) 1pb in same place as sl st, 1dc in next pb, [1pb in next dc, 1dc in next pb] x 9, 1pb in next dc, 1dc in 2pbtog, [1pb in next dc, 1dc in next pb] x 13, 1pb in next dc, 1dc in 2pbtog, [1pb in next dc, 1dc in next pb] x 3, sl st in first pb of rnd to close – 56sts (28pb, 28dc).

Rnd 15: (maintain stitch count) 1ch, 1dc in same place as sl st, [1pb in next dc, 1dc in next pb] x 27, 1pb in last dc, sl st into first dc of rnd 15 – 56sts (28pb, 28dc).

Rnd 16: (decrease)1pb in same place as sl st, 1dc in next pb, [1pb in next dc, 1dc in next pb] x 9, 2pbtog in next 3 sts, 1dc in next pb, [1pb in next dc, 1dc in next pb] x 12, 2pbtog in next 3 sts, 1dc in next pb, [1pb in next dc, 1dc in next pb] x 2, sl st in first pb in rnd – 52sts (24pb, 2 x 2pbtog and 26dc).

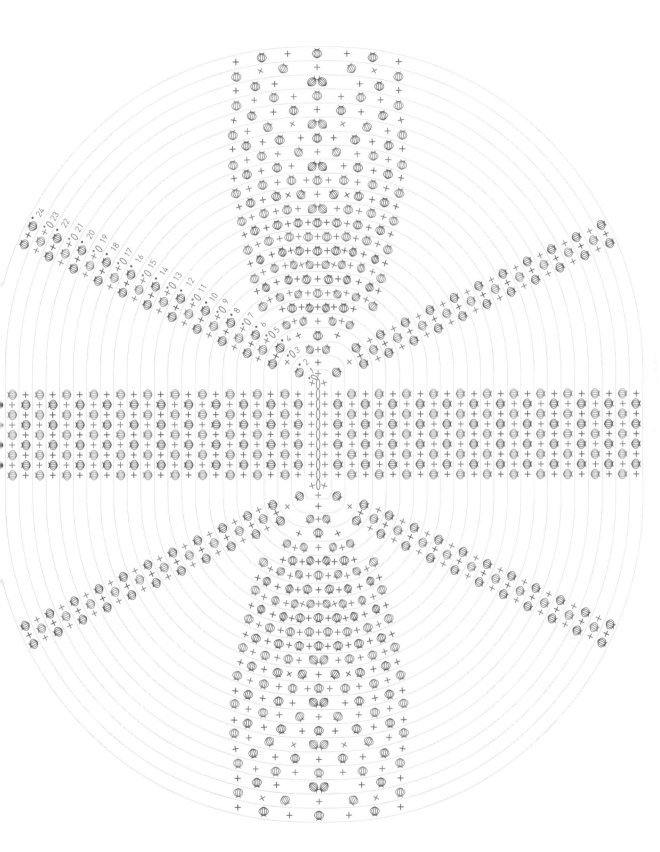

Rnd 17: (maintain stitch count) 1ch (does not count as first stitch), 1dc into same place as sl st, [1pb in next dc, 1dc in next pb] x 9, 1pb in next dc, 1dc in 2pbtog, [1pb in next dc, 1dc in next pb] x 12, 1pb in next dc, 1dc in 2pbtog, [1pb in next dc, 1dc in next pb] x 2, 1pb in last dc, sl st in first dc of rnd to close – 52sts (26pb, 26dc).

Rnd 18: (maintain stitch count) 1pb in same place as sl st, 1dc in next pb, [1pb in next dc, 1dc in next pb] x 25, sl st to first pb of rnd to close – 52sts (26pb, 26dc).

Rnd 19: (decrease) 1ch (does not count as first stitch), 1dc into same place as sl st, [1pb in next dc, 1dc in next pb] x 9, 2pbtog in next 3 sts, 1dc in next pb, [1pb in next dc, 1dc in next pb] x 11, 2pbtog in next 3 sts, 1dc in next pb, 1pb in next dc, 1dc in next pb, 1pb in next dc, sl st in first dc of rnd – 48sts (22pb, 2 x 2pbtog and 24dc).

Rnd 20: (maintain stitch count) 1pb in same place as sl st, 1dc in next pb, [1pb in next dc, 1dc in next pb] x 8, 1pb in next dc, 1dc in 2pbtog, [1pb in next dc, 1dc in next pb] x11, 1pb in next dc, 1dc in 2pbtog, [1pb in next dc, 1dc in next pb] x 2, sl st in first pb of rnd to close – 48sts (24pb, 24dc).

Rnd 21: (maintain stitch count) 1ch (does not count as first stitch), 1dc into same place as sl st, [1pb in next dc, 1dc in next pb] x 23, 1pb in last dc, sl st in first dc of rnd to close – 48sts (24pb, 24dc).

Rnd 22: (decrease) 1pb in same place as sl st, 1dc in next pb, [1pb in next dc, 1dc in next pb] x 8, 2pbtog in next 3 sts, 1dc in next pb, [1pb in next dc, 1dc in next pb] x 10, 2pbtog in next 3 sts, 1dc in next pb, 1pb in next dc, 1dc in next pb, sl st in first pb of rnd to close – 44sts (20pb, 2 x 2pbtog, 22dc).

Rnd 23: (maintain stitch count) 1ch (does not count as first stitch), 1dc into same place as sl st, [1pb in next dc, 1dc in next pb] x 8, 1pb in next dc, 1dc in 2pbtog, [1pb in next dc, 1dc in next pb] x 10, 1pb in next dc, 1dc in next pb, 1pb in last dc, sl st in first dc of rnd to close – 44sts (22pb, 22dc).

Rnd 24: (maintain stitch count – last puff ball round) 1pb in same place as sl st, 1dc in next pb, [1pb in next dc, 1dc in next pb] x 21, sl st in first pb of rnd to close – 44sts (22pb, 22dc).

Rnd 25: 1ch (does not count as first stitch), 1dc in same place as sl st, 1dc in each st around, sl st in first dc to close – 44dc. Fasten off.

Attaching the handles

How you attach your handles depends on the type you are using. The wooden handles illustrated here have a single narrow slot which I calculated to be 20dc wide. Laying the bag flat to establish where the edges were, I re-attached the yarn 1 stitch in from the edge and made an extended piece of crochet (20 stitches wide and 5 rows high) to the top of the bag on each side, which I fed through the slots in the handles and then crocheted back on itself to create a loop around the wood. (These extensions should have 2 stitches between them on each side.)

Lining

Make a lining for the bag once the crocheting is done so that you can cut it to fit. Fold the fabric in two, right side to right side. Lay the bag on the folded fabric with the fold along the bottom and draw around the bag. Cut along your drawn line. For a particularly puffy and fulsome lining, draw round your folded fabric piece onto a folded piece of quilter's wadding. Open the wadding and fabric pieces out and lay them together, the wrong side of the fabric next to the wadding. Then treat them as one thereafter. Folding right sides together again, and leaving a 1cm seam allowance, stitch down each side of the bag lining. Fold out the raw edge and press it. Put the lining inside the bag, pin the folded-over top to the top row of crocheting (not counting the extensions) and handstitch in place.

You'll find that the puff balls are voraciously yarn-hungry and will eat quickly through your stash, but their generous volume is key to this bag's colourful character.

Diamond Popcorn Cowl

The 5-post popcorns are worked into a striking diamond pattern on this chunky cowl. A stylish addition to your wardrobe, this cowl is also an interesting and easy project for practising your new-found skills. Choose a yarn that is comfortable next to your skin.

You will need

5mm crochet hook
Chunky yarn in blue/grey:
460m (504yd)

Abbreviations

A list of common abbreviations is given on page 94. Below are some special ones used for this project.
BPtr = back post treble (see 'Special stitches')
FPtr = front post treble (see 'Special stitches')
pc = 5-post popcorn (see 'Special stitches')

Tip

Front post and Back post stitches sound more complicated than they are. The only real difference between them and ordinary trebles is that instead of inserting your hook under the two loops at the top of the stitch, you insert it under the 'stem' or 'post' of the treble stitch. If you feel it's a 'step too far', you can use normal trebles in the round-the-post rows instead and you'll still get a beautiful cowl.

Pattern
SPECIAL STITCHES

Standard 5-post popcorn (pc) – see page 49.

Front post treble (FPtr) – yarn over, insert hook from the front, going into the right of the next stitch stem, moving from right to left behind the stitch and emerging at the front to the left of the stem, yarn over and pull a loop through, then yarn over and pull through 2 loops twice – as with the standard treble stitch.

Back post treble (BPtr) – yarn over, starting with the hook behind the work, insert to the right of the next stitch stem, moving from right to left in front of the stitch and emerging at the back to the left of the stem, yarn over and pull a loop through, then yarn over and pull through 2 loops twice – as with the standard treble stitch.

Ch 86, leaving about 10cm tail.

Rnd 1: 1tr in 4th ch from hook, 82tr, taking care not to twist the work, sl st last st to top of first 3ch, then use tail to join sts at their base; no need to turn – 84sts.

Rnd 2: (1FPtr, 1BPtr) x 42.

Rnd 3: 3ch (counts as first st), (1pc, 11tr) x 6, 1pc, 10tr, sl st into top of 3ch at beg of rnd, turn – 84sts (7pc, 77tr).

Rnd 4: 1 sl st, turn, 3ch (counts as first st), (1pc, 1tr, 1pc, 9tr) x 6, 1pc, 1tr, 1pc, 8tr, sl st into top of 3ch at beg of rnd, turn – 84sts (14pc, 70tr).

Rnd 5: 1 sl st, turn, 3ch (counts as first st), *(1pc, 1tr) x 2, 1pc, 7tr, repeat from * x 5, (1pc, 1tr) x 2, 1pc, 6tr, sl st into top of 3ch at beg of rnd, turn – 84sts (21pc, 63tr).

Rnd 6: 1 sl st, turn, 3ch (counts as first st), *(1pc, 1tr) x 3, 1pc, 5tr, repeat from * x 5, (1pc, 1tr) x 3, 1pc, 4tr, sl st into top of 3ch at beg of rnd, turn – 84sts (28pc, 56tr).

Rnd 7: 1 sl st, turn, 3ch (counts as first st), *(1pc, 1tr) x 4, 1pc, 3tr, repeat from * x 5, (1pc, 1tr) x 4, 1pc, 2tr, sl st into top of 3ch at beg of rnd, do not turn – 84sts (35pc, 49tr).

Rnd 8: 1 sl st, do not turn, 3ch (counts as first st), *(1pc, 1tr) x 3, 1pc, 5tr, repeat from *x 5, (1pc, 1tr) x 2, 1pc, 4tr, sl st into top of 3ch at beg of rnd, do not turn – 84sts (28pc, 56tr).

Rnd 9: 1 sl st, 3ch (counts as first st), *(1pc, 1tr) x 2, 1pc, 7tr, repeat from * x 5, (1pc, 1tr) x 2, 1pc, 6tr, sl st into top of 3ch at beg of rnd – 84sts (21pc, 63tr).

Rnd 10: 1 sl st, 3ch (counts as first st), (1pc, 1tr, 1pc, 9tr) x 6, 1pc, 1tr, 1pc, 8tr, sl st into top of 3ch at beg of rnd – 84sts (14pc, 70tr).

Rnd 11: 3ch (counts as first st), (1pc, 11tr) x 6, 1pc, 10tr, sl st into top of 3ch at beg of rnd, turn – 84sts (7pc, 77tr).

Rnds 12–19: As Rows 4–11 (no need to turn at end of Row 20).

Rnd 20: 3ch (counts as first st), 83tr, sl st in top of 3ch at close of round.

Rnd 21: As Row 2. Fasten off. Weave in ends.

Chart key

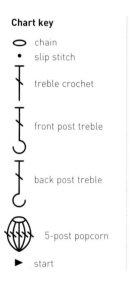

○ chain

• slip stitch

treble crochet

front post treble

back post treble

5-post popcorn

▶ start

Note

After the foundation chain the rest of the pattern is worked in continuous rounds. To conceal the joins on rounds where the diamond shape widens you will be turning the work momentarily in order to slip stitch into position, then re-turning to continue working round the same way as the round below.

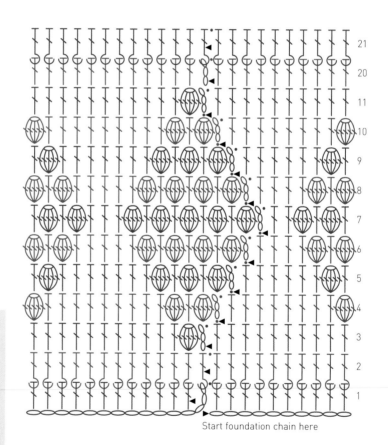

Start foundation chain here

Common Abbreviations

beg	beginning
ch	chain(s); also 'Work [a given number] of chains.'
cm	centimetre(s)
Col	colour
dc	double crochet
DK	double knitting (yarn)
dtr	double treble
foll	following, follows
htr	half treble
inc	including
m	metre(s)
Rnd	round
RS	right side
sk	skip
sl st	slip stitch
sp	space
st	stitch
tog	together
tr	treble
WS	wrong side
yd	yard(s)
yo	yarn over

Index

A

abbreviations 12, 13
  abbreviation key 14–15
  common abbreviations 94

B

back bumps 20
Bag, Puff Ball 86–90
blocking 27
bobbles 22, 32
  3-post bobbles 22, 32
  Bobble Berries 40
  Bobble Bumps 32, 39
  Bobdala 38
  Bricking 32, 34–35
  Diabobs 41
  getting the size right 24
  Granny Flower 36–37
  Long and Leaning 44–45
  Polkabobs 32, 42–43
  Puff Ball and Berry Rug 78–82
  Windmills 32, 46–47
  working a standard 3-post bobble 33
Bricked Puffs 62, 64
Bricking 32, 34–35
Bullion Stitch 62, 75

C

charts 13
  chart key 14–15
  common chart symbols 13
  using patterns and charts 14
colour, changing 19
Corn Rows 51
Cowl, Diamond Popcorn 91–93
crocheting together 29
  double crochet on the right side 29
  double crochet on the wrong side 29
  double crochet worked through both pieces 29
  double crochet zigzag seam 29
  making strips of blocks and joining in long seams 29
Cushion, Puff Bolster 83–85

D

decreasing 21
  decreasing by larger amounts 21
  decreasing by small amounts 21
  how to form a cluster decrease 21
Diabobs 41
Diamond Popcorn Cowl 91–93

Dipped Puffs 62, 65
double crochet 16
double treble 17
drawstring ring 18

F

fastening off 19
    end of the row 19
    making shapes or pictures with
        colour 19
    two- or three-colour stripe schemes
        19
finishing your work 26–27
    blocking 27
    joining 28–29
    keeping notes 26
    labelling swatches 26
    recording yarn information 26
    weaving in ends 27
Flopcorns 58–59

G

Granny Flower 36–37

H

half treble 17
hooks 10
    matching yarn weights and
        hooks 11

I

increasing 20
    increasing by large amounts 20
    increasing by small amounts 20

J

joining 28–29
    crocheting 29
    joining in new yarn 19
    sewing 28
    tips 28

L

labelling swatches 26
Long and Leaning 44–45

M

magic ring 18

N

notes 26

P

patterns 12
    abbreviations 12, 13, 14–15
    charts 13
    other written instructions 12
    stitch 'equations' 13
    using patterns and charts 14
Picorns 60
Polkabobs 32, 42–43
popcorns 23, 48
    5-post popcorns 23, 48
    Corn Rows 51
    Diamond Popcorn Cowl 91–93
    Flopcorns 58–59
    getting the size right 25
    Picorns 60
    Pop Circles 48, 53
    Popcorn Patterning 56
    Popcorn Peonies 57
    Popcorn Tulips 48, 61
    Popcorn with Ribs 48, 52
    Poptarsia 52–53
    Scattered Corn 48, 50
    working a standard 5-post popcorn
        49
projects 77
    Diamond Popcorn Cowl 91–93
    Puff Ball and Berry Rug 78–82
    Puff Bolster Cushion 83–85
    Puff Ball Bag 86–90
puffs 23, 62
    5-pass puff 23, 62
    Bricked Puffs 62, 64
    Bullion Stitch 62, 75
    Dipped Puffs 62, 65
    getting the size right 25
    Puff Ball and Berry Rug 78–82
    Puff Balls 70
    Puff Bolster Cushion 83–85
    Puff Chevron 62, 66
    Puff Cushion 68–69
    Puff Ball Bag 86–90
    Puffs of Air 67
    Puffs on the Side 71
    Solomon's Puffs 74
    Spiked Puffs 72–73
    working a standard 5-pass puff 63

R

reading patterns 12–15
ring of chains 18
Rug, Puff Ball and Berry 78–82

S

Scattered Corn 48, 50
sewing 28
    back stitch 28
    chain stitch 28
slip stitch 16
Solomon's Puffs 74
Spiked Puffs 72–73
stitches 16
    double crochet 16
    double treble 17
    half treble 17
    slip stitch 16
    stitch 'equations' 13
    treble 17

T

techniques 16
    basic stitches 16–17
    changing colour and joining in new
        yarn 19
    increasing and decreasing 20–21
    when (and when not) to fasten off 19
    working in the round 18
tension 24–25
treble 17
turning chain 12

W

weaving in ends 27
Windmills 32, 46–47
working in the round 18
    magic (drawstring) ring 18
    ring of chains 18
    working into the second chain 18

Y

yarns 10
    joining in new yarn 19
    matching yarn weights and hooks
        11
    recording yarn information 26

Credits

Photography of yarn ball band on inside cover flap is used courtesy of Debbie Bliss Yarn. Thanks to Ligne Roset for the locations on page 79 and 85. All other step-by-step illustrations and other images are the copyright of Quarto Publishing plc. While every effort has been made to credit contributors, Quarto would like to apologize should there have been any omissions or errors — and would be pleased to make the appropriate correction for future editions of the book.

Author's Acknowledgements

To my talented mum, Julie Rankin, whose crafting skills know no bounds, and who created the culture that nurtured my own. And to Howard and Gabriel, who gave me the time and space to make this book happen.

Video Tutorial Links

Each QR code, once scanned with your smartphone, will link to the tutorial for the crochet stitch listed beside it. Simply download a free app to scan, if needed, and check out the short videos to help you crochet the perfect bobble, popcorn and puff. Alternatively you can use the url link provided to access the films.

3-post bobble

http://qr.quartobooks.com/ppbc/clip1.html

5-post popcorn

http://qr.quartobooks.com/ppbc/clip2.html

5-pass puff

http://qr.quartobooks.com/ppbc/clip3.html